KITE FLIGHT

*Complete, easy-to-follow instructions
for making 40 different kites*

Jack Botermans and Alice Weve

KITE FLIGHT

Complete, easy-to-follow instructions for making 40 different kites

Text: Rob van den Dobbelsteen

Illustrations: Toon van der Struijk

Photography: David van Dijk

An Owl Book
HENRY HOLT AND COMPANY
New York

Published by Henry Holt and Company, Inc.,
521 Fifth Avenue, New York, New York 10175.

Originally published in The Netherlands under the title
Vliegers maken.

Library of Congress Cataloging Publication Data.
Botermans, Jack
Kite Flight
Translation of: Vliegers maken.
'An Owl Book'
1. Kites I. Title.
TL759.B68 1986   629.133'32   85-17641

ISBN: 0-03-008518-7 (pbk.)

First American Edition
Created by: Jack Botermans
Text: Rob van den Dobbelsteen
Models: Alice Weve
Illustrations: Toon van der Struijk
Photography: David van Dijk
Design: Jack Botermans

Printed in The Netherlands

10 9 8 7 6 5 4 3 2 1

ISBN 0-03-008518-7

CONTENTS

Kite flying in the past. On a dull spring day a gigantic box kite went up on the French estate of the Lartigue family. In those days kite flying was considered a very eccentric hobby for such a fabulously wealthy family.

INTRODUCTION

He was a photographer and was sent by this paper to Nassau to take pictures of a kite festival taking place there. When he came back he asked his editor never to send him again on such a boring mission. 'I'd prefer to take pictures of grass growing. It's more exciting', he said.

It's a pity he hadn't gone to Central India a few years before. The world championship for fighter kites took place there in the grounds of the hunting palace of the Maharajah of Bhavatpur. For three hours the kites, wheeling through the air, guided by the little finger or the index finger and covered with hooks, sharp spikes and splinters of glass glued onto the razor sharp strings, fought for the title. Finally the American kite flyer, Yolen, won with a brilliantly executed manoeuvre which massacred the Maharajah's kite by forcing it into the top of a tree.

India was dumbfounded to see the Maharajah defeated and an American take the championship. After all, kites had been flying in Asia since time immemorial. The best kites had always been made in Japan, China, Korea and India, and the people of Asia had always been by far the most skilful and adept at flying them. In 200 B.C. the Chinese general, Han Hsin, had managed to defeat a heavily defended city with the help of a kite.

The city was surrounded by walled fortifications and the soldiers were unable to scale them. After every attack they would retreat, licking their wounds, and it is hardly surprising that the general was not at all pleased. He decided to try burrowing his way under the wall, which meant digging a tunnel.

However, the art of surveying in those days was not very sophisticated and apparently the first attempt was a miserable failure. When the soldiers dug their way up at the end of the tunnel, they were still quite a way outside the city walls.

Then Hsin had the idea of using a kite to measure the distance. He flew the kite and let it out until it was more or less over the centre of the city. Then he marked the string and in this way found out what the lenght of the tunnel should be.

The city was successfully stormed and Han Hsin went down in history as one of the first generals to use a kite as a tactical weapon in warface. In fact, he was not actually the very first. This was probably Huan Theng, another Chinese general, who was cornered with his army and unable to find any means of escape. To break the siege Theng had a very clever idea, which has also found its way into the history books. In the middle of the night he let up a squadron of kites fitted with wind harps and flutes. These instruments made such an eerie sound above the enemy that they fled in terror to a safer and quieter place.

A Hamamatsu kite painted with the design of the terrifying Tengu, the Japanese giant of the mountains.

Readers who are familiar with Japanese characters will recognise the character on this kite which means dragon.

Finally, a Korean general once hung a lamp on the tail of a kite to inspire his army with new courage. His plan worked, for the soldiers thought the light was a star sent by God and they went into battle so fearlessy that they made mincemeat of the enemy within a few hours.

Thus Asia was undoubtedly where kite flying originated. The Venetian merchant, Marco Polo, was probably the first European ever to see a kite. He did not fail to notice that in some cases a human being was tied onto the kite, and he wrote some excited reports home to Venice about this – but he didn't specify whether it was a man or woman tied to the kite. Marco Polo was a brave man himself, but he assumed that the person must be a criminal condemned to 'flying', a drunk or an idiot, as no one in their right mind would take such a big risk.

Even a genius like Marco Polo could not see into the future. For the people who tried flying themselves, carried by a kite – an idea that was popular in various places in the world in the nineteenth century – were by no means mad. A Breton sailor, Jean le Bris, was one of the first to make the attempt, using a horse-drawn cart to pull the kite up into the air from a beach. This attempt took place in December 1856 and resulted only in a broken leg.

The British kite flyer, Sir George Caley, was not so lucky. This fanatic had constructed a double kite with a lift which surprised even him.

Shops

Photography shops were rather shocked a few years ago when people started to develop and print their own films. This was bound to lead to a fall in trade. Professional photographers, as those in the business were keen to call themselves, saw their own status begin to dwindle. However, as we all know, things were very different. Professional photographers are still around, and in fact business has increased rather than decreased, with customers coming in for the odd bottle of developing fluid, a box of photographic paper or a new lens for their camera. You may well ask what all this has to do with kites. Initially the professional kite builders, who sold kites in kites shops and were recognised as experts, were not over-enthusiastic about books like this one, which describe how to make kites yourself. Nevertheless, the same thing applies, and kite shops are doing better trade than ever.

This stands to reason. Not only can you admire all the wonderful materials for sale and be inspired by the imagination of the shopowners. In addition, the owner can give his customers all sorts of tips. Lastly, you can usually find a variety of materials which you need for kite building and which you would otherwise have to shop around for.

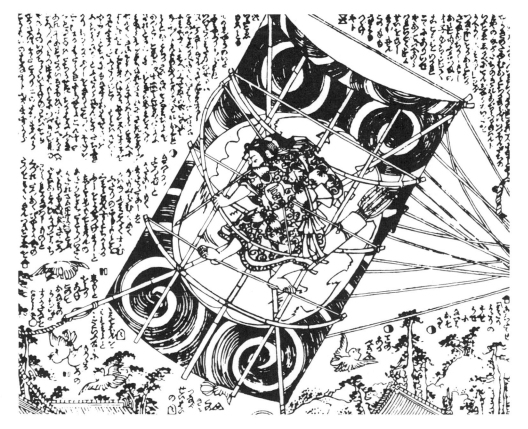

Japanese D-Day in the old days consisted of an invasion from the air. You may wonder what soldiers would prefer: to wade knee deep through the water to the beach – or, as in this case, being tied onto a kite (from a nineteenth century engraving).

He thought it might be possible to use it to glide over the valley of Brompton. However, he was obviously not quite certain of it and ordered his coachman to try out the contraption. The consequences were distastrous. Admittedly the coachman whirled from the east to the west of the valley – to the great satisfaction of Sir George himself, who had both feet firmly planted on the ground – but when Cayley enthusastically asked the coachman about the experience, the poor man could only say: 'I'm at your service, sir, but I resign. I was employed to drive a coach, not to fly'.

This put rather a damper on the celebration of what has been described as the first manned kite flight. (Cayley's coachman performed this party piece against his better judgment in 1853.) Sir George's invention was never used for a flight again. The idea of using a double kite fizzled out and remained in the background until it emerged once again at the end of the nineteenth century when the inventor of the telephone, the Scotsman Alexander Graham Bell, began experimenting with kites in a bay in Canada.

Bell's greatest triumph was a flight of seven minutes made by Lieutenant Thomas E. Selfridge of the American Army, above Baddeck Bay. Selfridge went up fifty metres in the kite built by Bell, which was pulled by a steamer. In 1907 this caused an immediate sensation. Nevertheless, Selfridge never became famous for this success. Nine month later he crashed in an aeroplane designed by the Wright brothers and broke his neck. The brave lieutenant was the first victim of motorised aviation.

The kite in which Selfridge made his flights was also more or less forgotten. It never became famous like the best known kite of all time, the kite used by Benjamin Franklin in 1752 to prove that electricity in lightning was the same as electricity on earth. Any self-respecting physics textbook has a picture of this American who shirked at nothing, conducting his extremely dangerous experiments.

Franklin thought he had taken some precautionary measures, for example, using a silk rope, but it is certainly never advisable to fly a kite during a thunderstorm. Of course, you can always use a glass reel, like the Swiss scientist, Dr. Colladon. In 1826 this young man nearly gave his father a heart attack by reproducing Franklin's experiment in the living room. As far as Colladon was concerned it was a resounding success; flashing of lightning over a metre long flashed through the living room, according to a biography of Colladon, but his father was less enthusiastic and ordered his son to bring the kite inside immediately, glass reel and all, for the experiment struck him as being more than a little dangerous.

Franklin, Bell and Colladon were by no means the only inventors to fly kites in the name of science. The Italian count, Guglielmo Marconi, used a kite to pull up the aerial which received the first wireless communication between Europe and America. Even today thermometers attached to kites are among the most

The assortment consists, of course, of more than scissors, glue and a little line. To build a good and especially reliable kite many appliances are needed. On the pages 14 to 17 everything that is needed has been described and supplied with the necessary instructions.

Now do not say that the Y-parts, rings and flexible cross joints are completely unnecessary, because Dad used to make kites without these things. You will see that these aids make the job easier and what is even more important, they will enable you to build a better kite.

Kite speciality shop. You cannot take your eyes off them.

Fighting kites are not only popular in the Far East: Here a picture taken at the beach of Scheveningen.

Tastes differ. But it cannot be denied that these hand painted silk bird or butterfly shaped kites are among the most beautiful in the world. They are really too beautiful to fly, for a start because they are not exactly inexpensive. However, they do not have to be made of silk. Bird and butterfly shaped kites of paper are nearly as beautiful as their sumptuous silk counterparts. They are also extremely suitable for decorative purposes. On the right a Chinese printing from the nineteenth century with several bird shaped kites.

important instruments available to meteorologists and they are used throughout the world. However, human nature being what it is, kites have also been used for more nefarious purposes. In 1689 a besieged town in Siam was forced to surrender when the besieging army used bombs tied to kites to bombard the town. It is also a well-known fact that during the Second World War some of the submarines in the German navy had an Autogino kite on board which was sent up as soon as the Germans needed to scout out the area.

On the other hand, kites were also used in more constructive ways, or at least various attempts were made in this direction. For example, someone had the bright idea that it would be possible to make use of a kite to take a lifeline to a shipwrecked ship and thus save the victims on board. Someone else had the

A picture found in any physics textbook at secondary school. Benjamin Franklin conducting his famous experiment which eventually resulted in the development of lightning conductors.

New reconnaissance techniques used by the British in about 1900. A reconnaissance instrument is sent up in the air over enemy territory using a man-carrying kite developed by Cody. The experiment was by no means an unqualified success. A few seconds after the shutter of the camera has clicked, the kite – plus the poor soldier taking the picture – plummeted into the sea. Fortunately he suffered no more than a severe soaking.

idea that a kite would be eminently suitable for transporting food and medicine to people who were stranded in a completely inaccessible place – the poor souls stranded on the above-mentioned shipwreck, to give just one example. Yet another came up with the by no means illogical notion of using a kite to lift radio antennae and telephone cables to places which would normally only be accessible to acrobats. However, it cannot be claimed that any of these brain-waves ever led to a thriving kite industry. Kites are very occasionally used for practical purposes, but in ninety-nine cases out of a hundred, kites go up in the air because the owners holding the strings enjoy flying them.

Unfortunately it is not often that a kite owner will fly his kite in the enthusiastic company of other kite fanatics, whether this is on the beach at Scheveningen, in Twente, or in the centre of Amsterdam. A few years ago a kite revival took place in the Netherlands, starting in the capital. The Amsterdam Balloon Society, a group of experts who had been studying the advantages of 'soft aviation' for some time, organised the first kite festival in Amsterdam. The kite festival was a much bigger success than the Balloon Society had dared to hope. A year later the festival had become an event where kites were not the only attraction, but where the crowds who had come to watch could also enjoy the performances of many different musicians, such as SNOB (a Dutch group), a ladies' choir, and a large orchestra. There were competitions for the most beautiful, the highest flying and the strongest kite; at times there were more than 100,000 spectators.

In addition some kites are sent up for quite different reasons. For example, in Korea and Malaysia, flying kites is considered to be a way of getting rid of all sorts of ailments and problems. Whether you are suffering from kidney stones, an upset tummy or a dreadful boss, a kite can deal with it. All you have to do is write the problem on the kite, fly it high, and then cut through the string. You can see your problem soaring up into the big blue sky and disappearing out of sight. But be warned: never pick up one of these kites when it has landed, otherwise you will then have the problem of dealing with the kidney stones, upset tummy or dreadful boss.

In these countries kites are also used – or misused, depending on your point of view – for driving out evil spirits. When a child is born, a sensible father immediately hurries to build a kite which not only resembles the newborn child, but which also bears the baby's name. It is believed that the evil spirit will concentrate on the kite and follow it as soon as the string is cut and the kite flies away. If this works, the child can be sure of a good life.

In conclusion, kites are used for a variety of purposes – to conquer an enemy, as a tool of science, to secure a prosperous future for a newborn child. Apart from all this, kiteflying can also provide you with hours of fun. You can become quite passionate about kite flying and kite construction. However, beware of going as far as the unhappy character in one of Somerset Maugham's famous stories, *The Kite*. This man preferred to rot in a damp dark dungeon rather than pay a penny of alimony to his former wife. Rather excessive, even though his wife had cut his favorite kite in two.

Anatomy

One or two anatomical tips. It's all fairly simple, as a kite consists of very few parts. But you should know what the long spar, the ventral keel and the bridle are. The illustrations show all these.

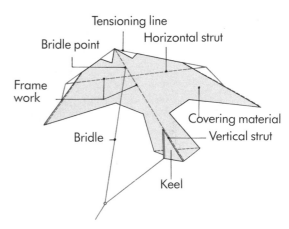

The different parts of a kite.

Every year increasingly large kite festivals are being organised all over the world. These are not only events where the most beautiful or the most daring creations are being judged, but they also serve as a place for an exchange of ideas regarding kite building.

Here we see Alice busily controlling Nick
Morse's Tetra variation.

15

TOOLS

It is no easy matter to build a kite with your bare hands — in fact, you could say that it was impossible. If you do try you'll inevitably encounter great obstacles, and you'll never end up with the kite you imagined to begin with. As in any other sort of construction work, good tools are half the battle when you're making a kite.

The question remains what tools a kite builder needs, and there are different opinions on this matter. A fanatic who spends all his time building kites might have more tools than the average carpenter. Obviously there is no need to go this far, and the following straightforward tools will enable anyone to build a kite without encountering too many difficulties.

1. Utility knife
2. Hand drill
3. Revolving perforator
4. Tongs to make eyelets
5. Trimming shears
6. Pincers
7. Small saw
8. Tape measure
9. Metal ruler
10. Domestic scissors
11. Pencil or fine felt tip pen
12. Pinking shears
13. Set square
14. Awl
15. Wood or hobby glue
16. Compasses

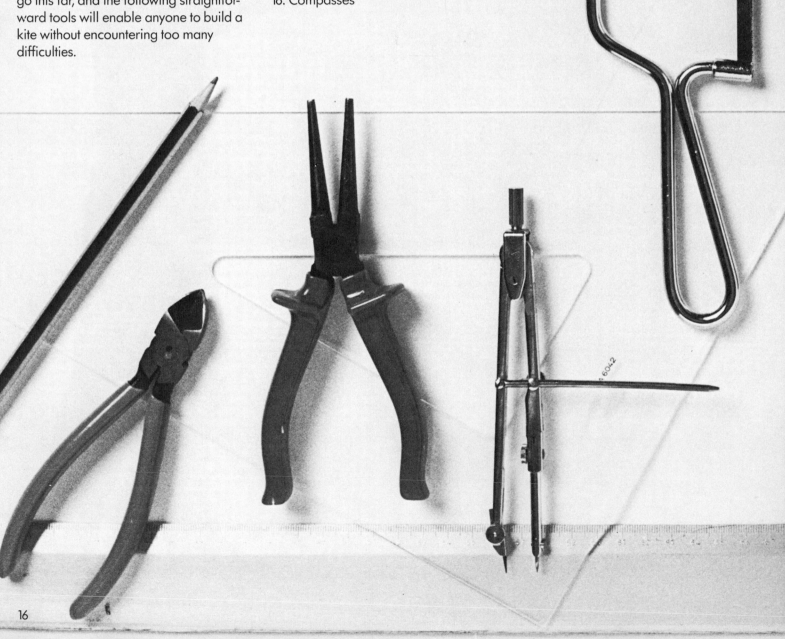

You can make it as complicated as you wish.
But any kite in this book can be built with the
tools shown here.

Rubber tips.
Rubber tips or plastic caps are essential for a properly finished kite. They add the perfect

professional touch when they are placed on the ends of the cross bars. However, this is not the only purpose for which you will need them.

Rubber tips are also very useful for securing the flying line on the ends.

Connecting pieces.
Left, a plastic nut used to attach the frame onto the stick.
Right, a plastic nut which enables you to fit propellors on the kite.

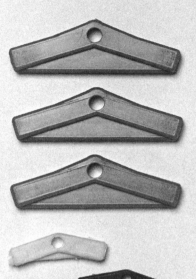

A few other possible variations. These are the connecting pieces used for fibreglass rods. Though there is no reason why they couldn't be used on thin wooden rods.

Flexible cross connection.
Some people want everything to be collaps-ible: deckchairs, bicycles, and even kites. They'll soon find that a flexible cross connection is essential for a collapsible kite. This shows an example with the rods that are connected.

Rigid cross connections.
As any technically minded person will know, a rigid cross connection is the opposite of a flexible cross connection.

Connections.
These +, Y and T junctions are virtually indispensible. They can be used both with wood and fibreglass (which have to be

An instrument without a name.
Invaluable to anyone wishing to make cross connections with fibreglass rods.

pushed into these pieces), but it is also quite possible to slide some aluminium tubes over them.

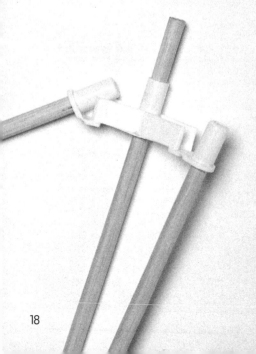

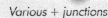

Various + junctions

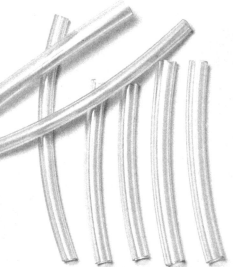

PVC-tubing.
Believe it or not, it's possible to build a kite using PCV-tubing. It's suitable for all sorts of purposes. With a hole punch you can even make cross connections but it's also possible to attach them directly to the canvas.

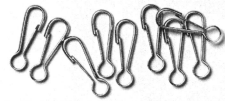

Swivel hook/clip.
Thank heaven for the person who invented the swivel hook. It is used when one piece has to be attached quickly to another piece.

Umbrella ends.
Umbrella ends are a very sophisticated piece of equipment. Note the hole, which provides all sorts of possibilities for the kite builder.

Caps.
Plastic caps on the rods. The rope is pulled through the slit and then capped.

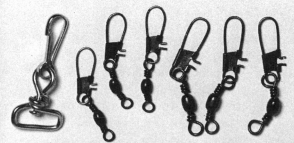

Swivels.
When the line turns, the swivel prevents the kite from turning as well.

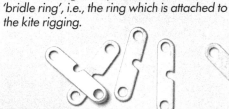

Rings.
A box of aluminium rings is always useful, even if the ring is only used as a so-called 'bridle ring', i.e., the ring which is attached to the kite rigging.

Tension adjusters.
These are familiar to campers, who use them to tighten guy ropes. They are also invaluable to a kite builder.

D-rings, normally used for curtains.

Key rings. On various points of the kite they are very suitable as tow ring, but also as connecting or coupling ring.

Ground anchor.
Whoever has hurt his hands once, because the kite was tugging at the line that hard, will from then on use a ground anchor to attach the line to.

THE FRAME

If you ask an amateur what a kite is made of, ninety-nine times out of a hundred he will answer with a triumphant grin: 'Wood, paper and string'. Wonderful, but on the other hand, no self-respecting jury would award this answer ten out of ten. In these enlightened times there are many materials on the market which seem almost purpose-made for the modern kite builder.

Starting with the skeleton or frame, it is admittedly true that this is still often made with strips of wood, particularly bamboo or wooden dowls which can be found in various lengths and thicknesses in hardware and art supply stores. Bamboo, available from any garden shop, is especially popular, but strips of pine, whitewood and ash are also excellent.

However, if you are thinking of building a larger than average kite, the best material is aluminium or fibreglass. The latter has the advantage of being as flexible as a circus acrobat. However, a disadvantage is that although it is easy to work with, it can easily splinter when you saw through it. Splinters can lodge in your skin or even find their way into the respiratory system, so great care should always be taken.

The thickness of the strips of wood depends entirely on the size of the kite (and the pressure that is therefore exerted on it) but in general it can be said that strips with a diameter of under 0,12 inch are too thin. The connections between the various strips are another story.

Flexible cross connection.
An example of a flexible cross connection using two pieces of tubing which have been cut through halfway.

Certainly string is still used, but it is by no means the easiest material to use.
You may well ask what works better – a cleverly knotted length of string or a piece of plastic tubing.
Plastic tubing is one of the many materials which can be used to join the long spar (vertical bar) with the cross spar (the horizontal bar). It is made from one of the many synthetic products which seem almost perfect for building kites.

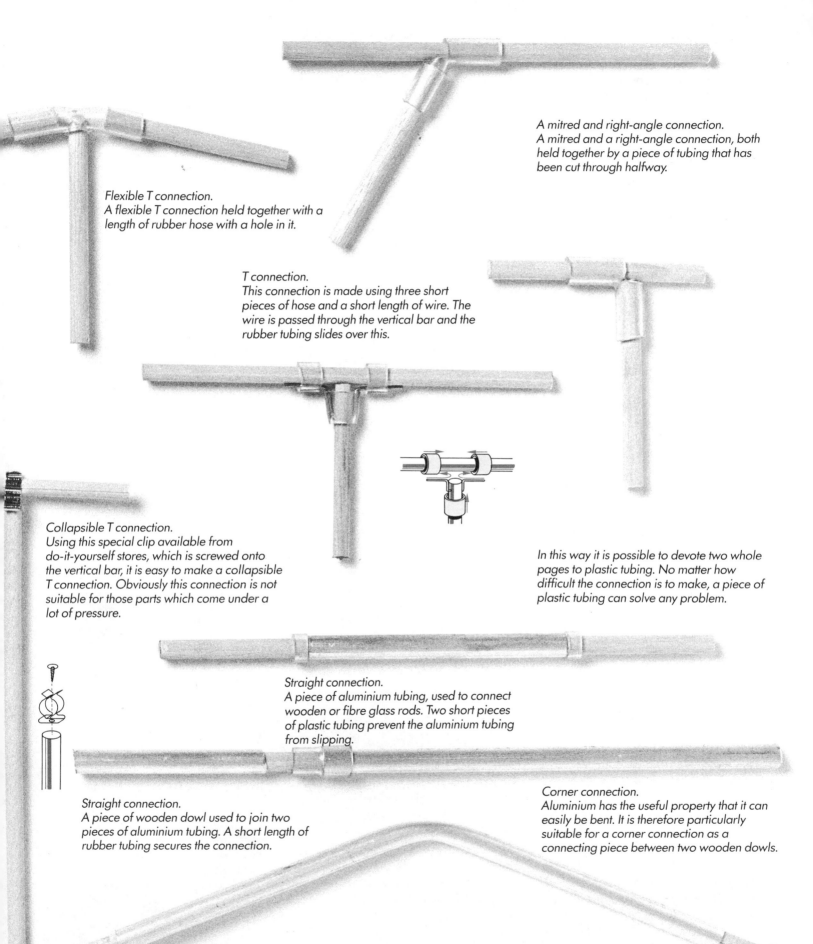

A mitred and right-angle connection.
A mitred and a right-angle connection, both
held together by a piece of tubing that has
been cut through halfway.

Flexible T connection.
A flexible T connection held together with a
length of rubber hose with a hole in it.

T connection.
This connection is made using three short
pieces of hose and a short length of wire. The
wire is passed through the vertical bar and the
rubber tubing slides over this.

Collapsible T connection.
Using this special clip available from
do-it-yourself stores, which is screwed onto
the vertical bar, it is easy to make a collapsible
T connection. Obviously this connection is not
suitable for those parts which come under a
lot of pressure.

In this way it is possible to devote two whole
pages to plastic tubing. No matter how
difficult the connection is to make, a piece of
plastic tubing can solve any problem.

Straight connection.
A piece of aluminium tubing, used to connect
wooden or fibre glass rods. Two short pieces
of plastic tubing prevent the aluminium tubing
from slipping.

Straight connection.
A piece of wooden dowl used to join two
pieces of aluminium tubing. A short length of
rubber tubing secures the connection.

Corner connection.
Aluminium has the useful property that it can
easily be bent. It is therefore particularly
suitable for a corner connection as a
connecting piece between two wooden dowls.

21

KITE STRING

If you didn't know any better, you might just walk into a shop and buy a hundred yards of string. After all, it is the kite that matters, not a silly piece of string which is really more of an afterthought. Woe betide any kite flyer who still thinks like this. Don't worry – we won't bamboozle you with deceleration factors, breaking strain or friction at great height. But to make sure that you don't buy a string without having the kite to use it with, a few words of advice on this subject – which is actually very important – are in order.

What quality line should be used? It's not easy to answer this question because it depends on a large number of different factors. If you really want to fly the kite properly, you should use a different quality of line in different wind conditions. In general it may be said that it's best to use the thinnest possible line – in other words, a line that won't break when the kite goes up. Obviously it requires experience to judge this, but by now the reader will have realized that kite flying is not as simple as it seems at first.

Therefore you start with the thinnest possible line. It is necessary to take into consideration not only the force of the wind, i.e., wind conditions, but also the size of the kite. Again this is a question of experience, but in this case there is a general rule that can be applied. Kite flying enthusiasts have always followed the rule that the tensile breaking strain of the line should be about fifteen times the surface area of the kite. For example, if the area of the kite is half a square yard, make sure that you choose a line with a breaking strain of at least $0.5 \times 33 = 16.5$ lb.

However, it should be pointed out that this is not a hard and fast rule. When there is a strong wind the breaking strain should certainly be greater, even though it is actually rather exciting to fly a kite on a line that is at 'snapping point'. An experienced kite flyer will feel from the reel what to do. If he suddenly feels the line go taut in a gust of wind, he must let out the line immediately; if there is not so much pull, the kite should be reeled in a little. It's rather like fishing. Always treat the string with great care and never step on it if it is lying on the ground for any reason. Before you know what's happening, you'll see your kite disappearing over the horizon.

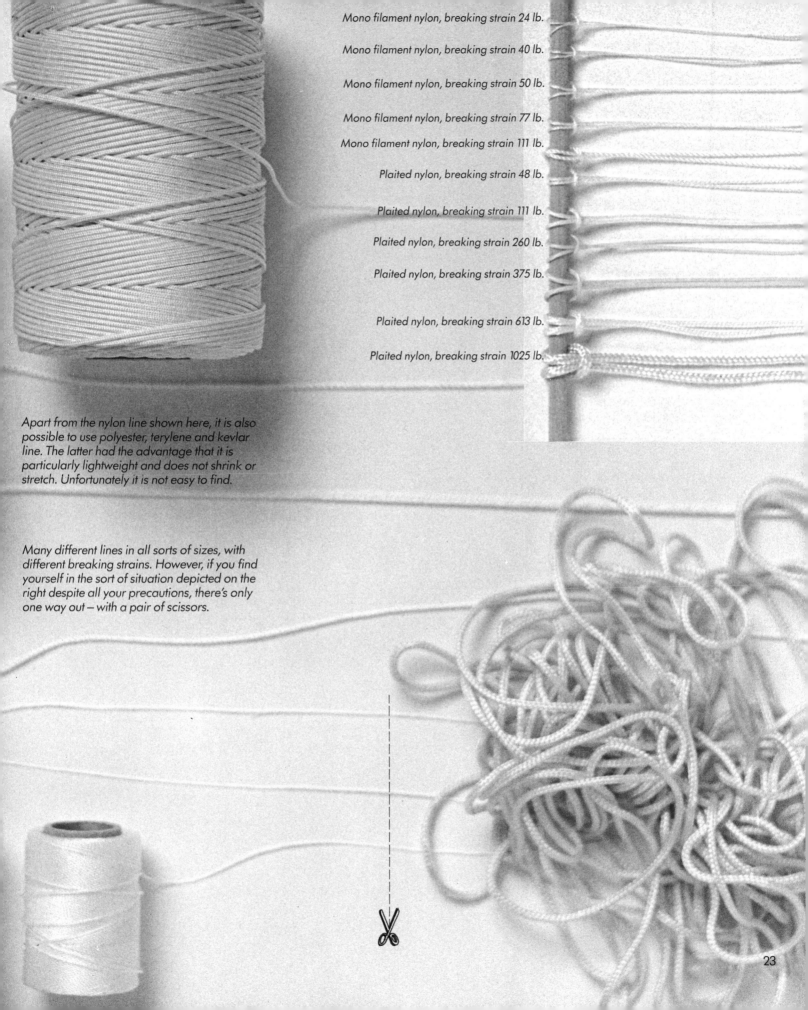

Mono filament nylon, breaking strain 24 lb.

Mono filament nylon, breaking strain 40 lb.

Mono filament nylon, breaking strain 50 lb.

Mono filament nylon, breaking strain 77 lb.

Mono filament nylon, breaking strain 111 lb.

Plaited nylon, breaking strain 48 lb.

Plaited nylon, breaking strain 111 lb.

Plaited nylon, breaking strain 260 lb.

Plaited nylon, breaking strain 375 lb.

Plaited nylon, breaking strain 613 lb.

Plaited nylon, breaking strain 1025 lb.

Apart from the nylon line shown here, it is also possible to use polyester, terylene and kevlar line. The latter had the advantage that it is particularly lightweight and does not shrink or stretch. Unfortunately it is not easy to find.

Many different lines in all sorts of sizes, with different breaking strains. However, if you find yourself in the sort of situation depicted on the right despite all your precautions, there's only one way out – with a pair of scissors.

23

KNOTS

Yes, we were going to talk about knots.
A tightly drawn loop or other string concoction
is something that has to be taken seriously.
You don't make a knot just like that. Take care:
the knot is always a weak spot in the line.
You must, therefore, take great care when you
make a knot and follow the rules we give
here. If you don't do that, it could cost you
your kite. This is a lesson to take in carefully
and remember.

1. This knot is what you need for attaching the
   line to the kite (i.e. to the balance).

2. If it is not for nothing that this knot is said to
   be 'as strong as a bear.'

3. A reef knot. If you are using strings of
   different thickness, use a reef knot.

4. Anybody who is making kites has to be
   able to do this one blindfold. You use this
   knot also when making the kite because it
   is quick and easy.

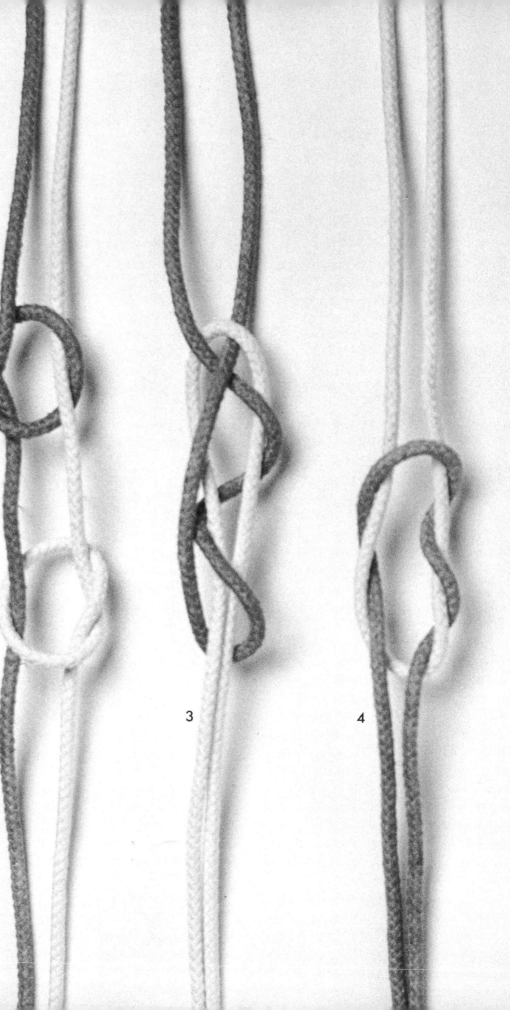

1   2   3   4

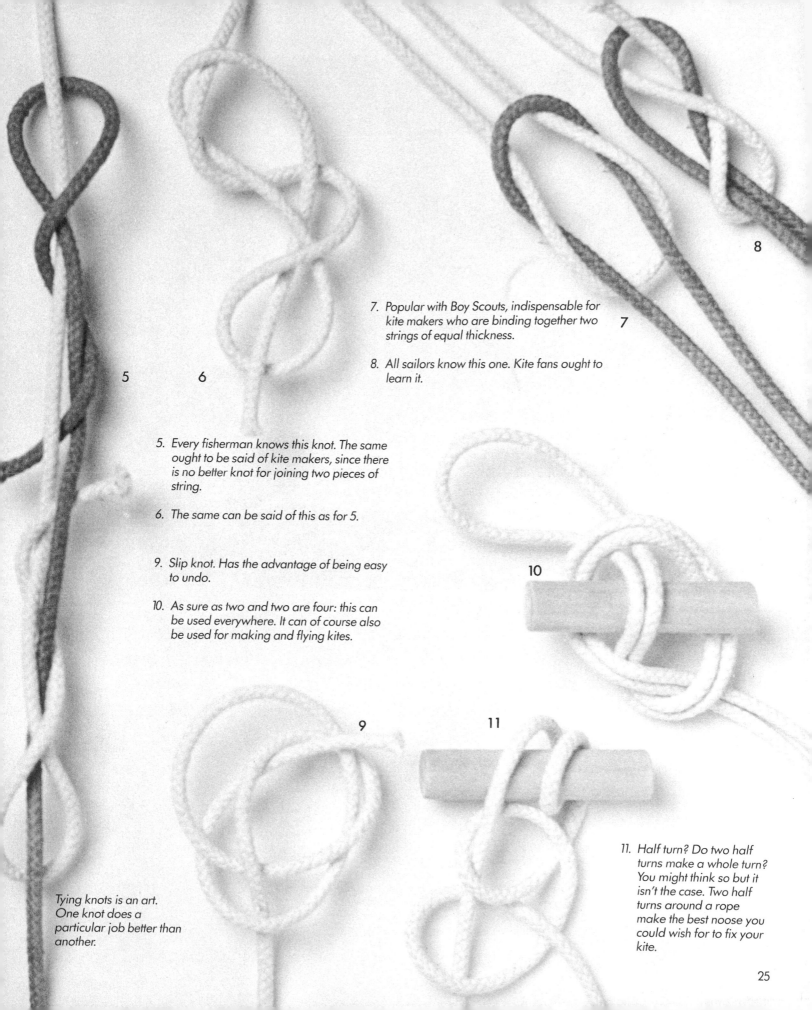

7. Popular with Boy Scouts, indispensable for kite makers who are binding together two strings of equal thickness.

8. All sailors know this one. Kite fans ought to learn it.

5. Every fisherman knows this knot. The same ought to be said of kite makers, since there is no better knot for joining two pieces of string.

6. The same can be said of this as for 5.

9. Slip knot. Has the advantage of being easy to undo.

10. As sure as two and two are four: this can be used everywhere. It can of course also be used for making and flying kites.

Tying knots is an art. One knot does a particular job better than another.

11. Half turn? Do two half turns make a whole turn? You might think so but it isn't the case. Two half turns around a rope make the best noose you could wish for to fix your kite.

25

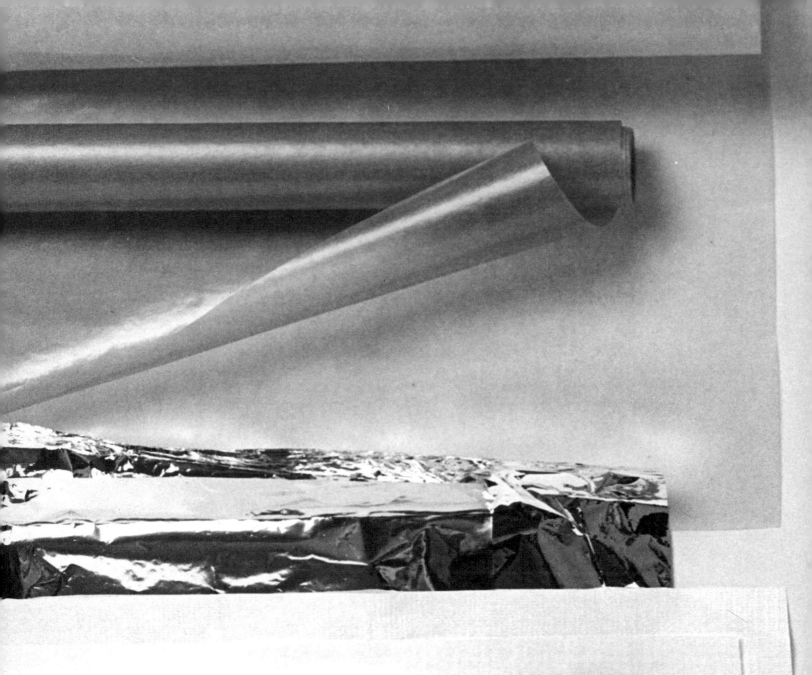

All sorts of materials can be used on the frame of the kite, from the familiar kite paper to advanced spinnaker fabric, from modern PVC to common newspaper. All these materials are suitable for kite construction as long as you bear in mind the expectations you have of your kite.

MATERIALS TO COVER THE KITE

The kite has a skin or covering, but in the past little thought was given to this aspect. You could simply buy kite paper by the square yard in toyshops. If you didn't have the money for real kite paper, you could use wrapping paper, which was cheaper or could even be obtained for nothing. Of course, it was only to be expected that this sort of skin would tear from time to time.

Even so, this traditional material should not be simply thrown overboard. It is still very suitable, though of course modern and stronger materials such as plastic are also available nowadays. There are different qualities and grades of plastic, and for kites polythene is the most suitable. It's not only strong, but is also relatively cheap. And it shouldn't be forgotten that polythene is available in all sorts of bright or pastel colours.

When it's possible to buy tyvek you're really in luck. This synthetic material was invented comparatively recently. It can be sown and glued, you can colour it any way you like, and it's not expensive. It's particularly good for folding kites, which is also true of nylon.

Perhaps you've seen a sailing boat, sailing before the wind with the balloon. Balloon spinnakers are made of spinnaker nylon, and it stands to reason that this material is also perfect for building a kite. Other suitable materials include very fine cotton, silk — though this is by no means cheap — and even linen.

Hemmed and stitched spinnaker cloth.

Hemmed and stitched tyvek.

Hemmed and stitched kite paper.

Tape for hemming the kite.

Tension cord which can be used for sticking the material onto.

27

STRETCHING TECHNIQUES

As modern materials such as spinnaker cloth and tyvek do not need cord for attaching the material, a few stretching techniques are described below in which the material is attached directly onto the kite frame.

1. A technique using press studs, which are suitable for attaching the material onto the frame in a number of places.

2. A method of attaching the material using a small keyring which fits into a groove cut into the end of a rod.

3. The same as 2, but in this case an extra ring is used to which the bridle is attached.

4. This is the easiest. An old-fashioned button fixed on the end of the material. The button fits into a groove cut into the end of a rod.

5. This method is oftern used for tents. A small piece of the material is sewn onto a corner of the rest of the material in such a way that the end of a rod fits exactly into it.

6. The same principle as 5 but in this case another ring is attached to the corner of the double stitched material so that other connections can also be made.

7. A length of PVC tubing that is attached to the material using a hole punch. The rod is then put into the rubber tubing.

8. A length of PVC tubing that is 'rolled' into the material and then stuck down. If a hole is then made in the tubing, a rod can be inserted into it.

9. Velcro sewn onto the end of the material is perfect for stretching the material tautly over the rods.

New materials make it possible to attach the material directly to the frame without using any cord or thread to sew them. A few examples are shown on this page.

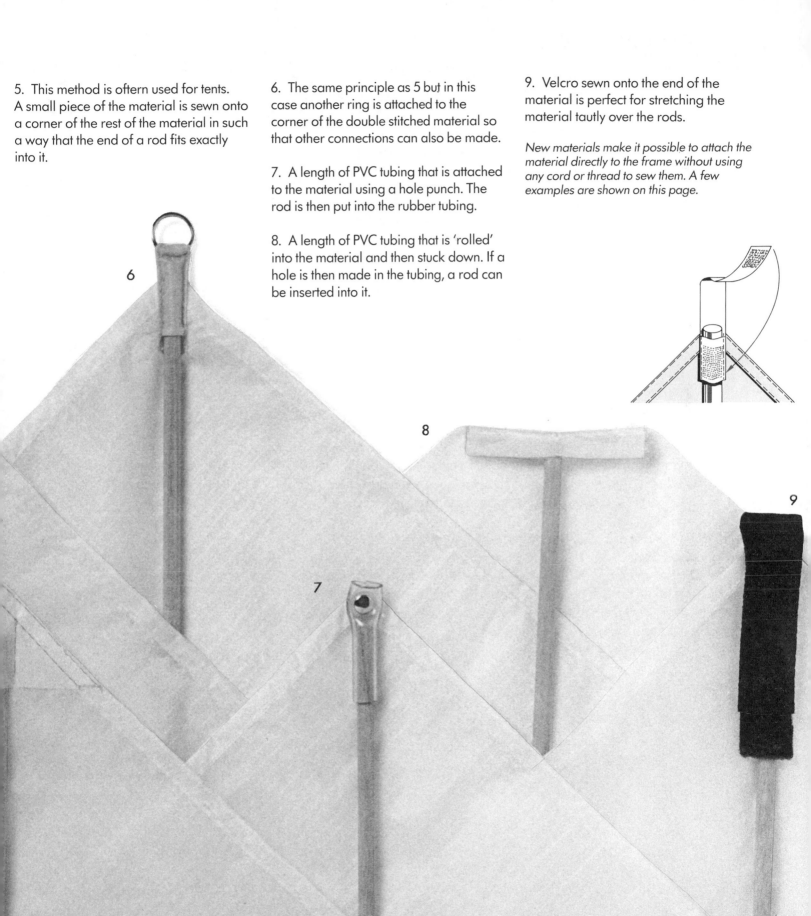

THE CLASSIC KITES

When people imagine a kite, most of them immediately think of the Malayan kite, although this particular kite has been known by many other names throughout the ages. Sometimes it is called the Javanese kite, the diamond kite, or even the classic kite. This kite has been flown for hundreds of years, but it was a fairly long time before it was introduced in the west for the simple reason that no one realised that the cross-spar had to be bowed. Travellers had seen kites flown by natives which seemed like statues in the firmament above the jungle. They were able to describe these kites in detail but they didn't realise that the Malayan kite would never leave the ground unless the cross-spar were curved. This was because the owners of the kites untied the strings from the cross-spars as soon as they brought them down. This was not because they wished to conceal the method of construction from the strangers, but simply to ease the tension on the cross-spar.

The American journalist and meteorologist, William Eddy, finally solved the mystery. He needed a stable kite for his meteorological observations and had heard stories about the Malayan kite which suggested that this type of kite would be suitable for his purposes. He finally managed to find an original kite in 1893 after searching for many years. It then took him a long time before he realised that the cross-spar had to be bowed if the kite were not to crash straight down to the ground after being prepared for take off.

Unaware of Eddy's discovery, Gilbert Totten Woglom performed quite a feat with the same sort of kite — which he called a 'Para Kite' — at more or less the same time. On 21 September 1895 he tied a camera onto his Para Kite and claimed to have taken the first aerial photograph of the western hemisphere with this device. However, this claim was violently disputed by E.D. Archibald, who stated that he had already done this in 1887.

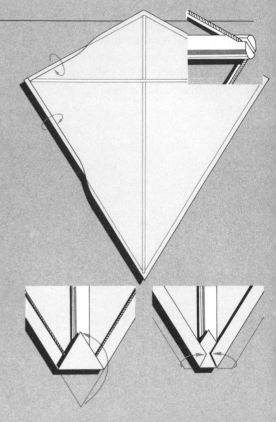

Construction using paper.
The best size for the kite is 1.1 × 0.8 yards, but there are people who have made the diamond 4.5 yards high. Join together two rods 1.1 yard and 0.8 yards long in the shape of a cross and then cut grooves 0.1 inch deep at the ends of the rods. Then tie a string through these grooves, lay the frame on a sheet of paper and cut round it, leaving a border of about 0.8 inch. First fold over the corners, then the hem, and glue them down. It is possible to bend the cross-spar using another string. The kite then needs a tail. The length of the tail depends on the wind speed.
The bridle should be attached as shown in the illustration. It's sometimes a good idea to reinforce the paper at the bridle points with some tape.

Construction with spinnaker sail.
First cut the cloth in the required shape. If there is to be a hem, allow ⅖ inch, but it's not absolutely necessary to hem this material. If it is not hemmed, cut out the pattern with a soldering iron. The edges melt and are finished off in this way. The

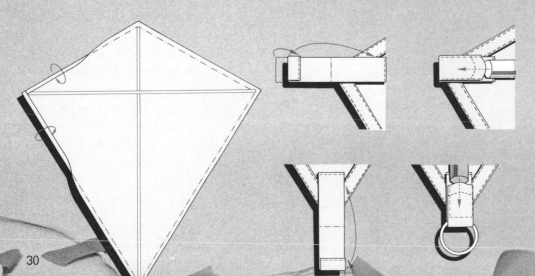

corners should be made as shown in the illustration. Then make the frame by sawing the rods to size and placing them in the corners of the material. The point where the rods cross can easily be fixed with a piece of cord. If desired, rings can be attached to the top and bottom of the fabric for attaching the bridle.

The most familiar type of kite: the classic kite. It is also known as the Malay-kite and the diamond kite, and probably by many other names as well.

STAR KITES

The sun is setting in the west, a train rumbles by in the distance, the frogs are croaking in the reeds and there's hardly a breath of wind. What can you do in these circumstances? It's hardly good kite flying weather. However, it may still be possible to fly a star kite, for there are people who think that a star kite will soar up if you just blow on it. Of course, this is an exaggeration, but it is true that a star kite needs little more than a slight breeze, and in fact prefers this. A strong wind certainly doesn't suit it.

This kite is based on the Indonesian star kite, though it is by no means as aggressive and is a lot easier to build. You could even just build a star kite as a decorative object to hang on a wall. On the other hand, you don't really build kites just to stick them up on the wall above your bed, however beautiful they may be. It cannot be denied that a star kite is a beautiful object, and it's one on which you can use all your inventiveness and creativity. You can make a five pointed or a six pointed star. You can give the kite an identity, such as the sun, for example, or starfish. And finally, you can either hang it up or fly it.

However, it's always best to fly it, especially if you've made a really beautiful one. The sun is setting in the west, a train rumbles by in the distance, frogs are croaking in the reeds and there's hardly a breath of wind. What can you do in these circumstances? You can fly your star kite.

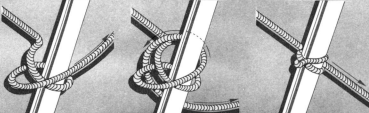

Building a five pointed star.
This five pointed star kite is made of paper. The construction method is identical to that of the classic kite. The size is 20 × 20 inch. Three rods 20 inch long are joined together as shown in the illustration. Join four points of the star with cord (see illustration).
Lie the frame on the paper and cut out the paper pattern, allowing about ¾ inch for a hem. First stick down the corners and then turn over the hem. You can decorate

the kite in an attractive way by sticking paper brushes to the ends of the rods. The bridle should be attached as shown in the illustration.
Building a six-pointed star.
This six-pointed star is made out of spinnaker material. First cut out the six pointed pattern as shown in the illustration. The distance between the points of the star should be 2 ft. Then hem round the edges of the fabric. Make an attachment for the rods at the ends

(described in detail on pp. 28-29). The inside corners should be reinforced with a piece of spinnaker material (see illustration). Now fit the rods and secure the point where they intersect by stitching a piece of tape to the material, which can then be tied round the rods. Obviously some decorative brushes can also be stuck onto this kite. You can bridle the kite in two places (see example) but with an extra bridle in the centre the six-pointed star kite can be used as a fighter kite.

Fixing the bridle

The star kite needs more than a little wind.

Fixing the bridle.

33

THE TUKKAL

The Tukkal is the mystery of Indian kite flying. Where does it come from? How old is it? As soon as the Tukkal gracefully takes to the air, the discussions begin. Kite experts always observe these kites with their eyes screwed up, deep lines of thought furrowed on their brows, but they rarely come out with anything more than: 'It's been around for seven hundred years'.

A kite flying pedant would be inclined to say: 'That's all very well and good, but it doesn't get me any further'. It remains a mystery, rather an exciting mystery, a mysterious kite which is great fun to fly, despite the fact that it is very obviously descended from the capricious Indian fighter kite.
The Tukkal feels so right because of its tailpart. The flexible tailpart gives the kite its stability, but still makes it suitable for a fighter kite. Obviously this requires some training on the part of both the kite and the kite flyer. You have to learn to control it and know exactly what it's going to do in particular conditions. But even when you know all this, the Tukkal can be very naughty. After all, it is a mystery.

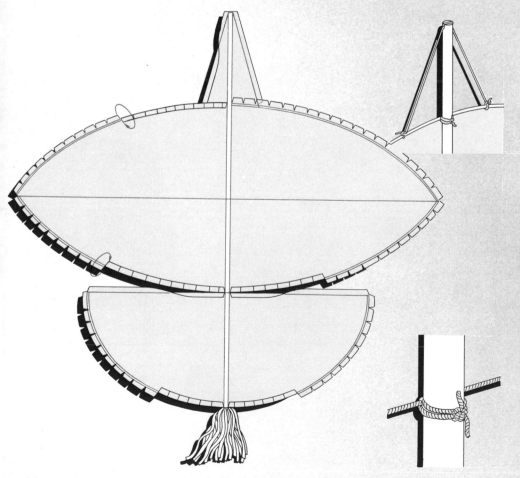

Traditional construction of bamboo and paper.
The kite is 1 yard 3.4 inch tall and 1 yard 3 inch wide. You will need four bamboo sticks: three thin ones 1 yard 3.4 inch long and one thicker one the same length. The thin bamboo sticks are used for the wings and should come to a point at the ends. For the large wings, first make the points by joining the ends of two sticks together, then pull them apart in the middle and fix

The Tukkal: the mystery kite from India.

them onto the thicker bamboo stick with some cord. The other bamboo stick is for the tail and should be stretched with a cord which is attached to the bottom of the thick bamboo stick. Allow 8 inch at the top of the thick bamboo stick and 4 inch at the bottom. Make an incision in the top of the thick stick, pass a cord through it and attach this to the top wing (see example). Lie the frame on a sheet of paper and cut out the shape allowing 8 inch for the hem. The point which will form the top of the kite can be cut out separately, as you otherwise waste a lot of paper. Make some cuts into the hem, fold over and stick down. If you use thissue paper, moisten it slightly before sticking it down so that it will eventually be tautly stretched over the frame. To complete the Tukkal, stick on a typically Indian brush as a tail.

Fixing the bridle

THE YAKKO

The Yakko is certainly one of the most beautiful Japanese kites. Scores of kite makers in the land of the rising sun are completely obsessed with this model, particularly as it lends itself to all sorts of fantastic and bizarre creations. Flapping in the wind, the Yakko can even change shape, for example, when the kite folds double in a particular place.

The Yakko was the footman of the Samurai, the legendary Japanese knights famous throughout the world for their peerless courage, ingenuity, toughness, loyalty, and often their original fighting skills in the service of their lord.
In addition, the Samurai lifestyle has even permeated present day Japanese society.
The Yakko, or footman kite, does not play any role in one of the best known Japanese legends, which involves both a Samurai and a kite. This kite was the Hachijo kite, named after the island where Minamoto-no-Tametomo and his son were exiled in the dim and distant past.
Tametomo, a famous Samurai and certainly no fool, considered the presence of his son so unnecessary in that desolate place that he built a gigantic kite to carry his heir to the mainland. It was a daring feat, demonstrating once again the indomitable ingenuity of the Samurai.
Their 'Yakkos' or footmen were usually similarly ingenious — one of the reasons why the Samurai tradition is so popular with the Japanese youth of today.
The Yakko kite also happens to be the most popular kite with Japanese children.

The traditional construction of the Yakko using modern materials.
The kite is 1 yard 3 inch tall and 1 yard 8.5 inch wide. You need three pieces of fibreglass, each 1.5 yard 6 inch long (diameter fibreglass ⅛ inch). These three rods are bound together with cord as shown in the illustration.
Lie the frame on the tyvek and cut out the pattern allowing 0.6 inch for the hem. The ends of the sleeves are cut in a rectangular shape and the points of the rectangle are folded into the centre of the curve (see illustration). Now turn over the hem all the way round and stick down. The bridle is in three sections and should be attached as shown in the illustration. This kite can be beautifully decorated using the ideas on these pages as examples.

Fixing the bridle.

The Yakko is one of the most popular
Japanese kites, particularly as it lends itself to
the most fantastic and bizarre creations.

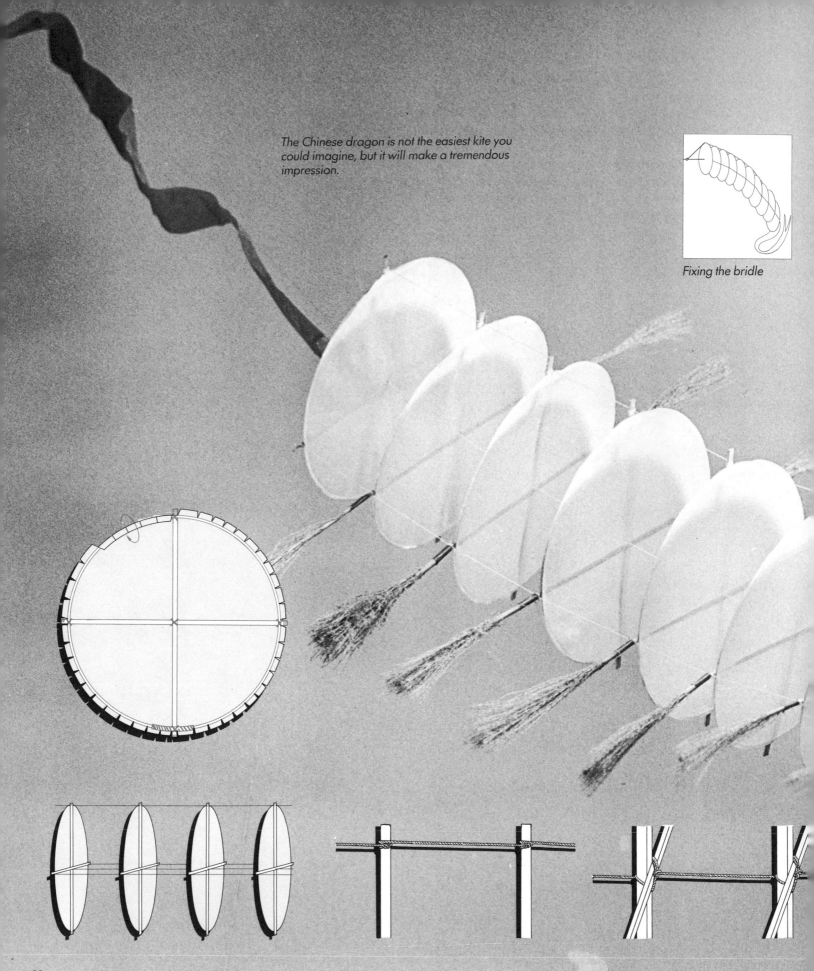

The Chinese dragon is not the easiest kite you could imagine, but it will make a tremendous impression.

Fixing the bridle

THE CHINESE DRAGON

This is a kite for real kite enthusiasts. It is variously known as the Chinese Dragon, the Chinese Snake and the Chinese Centipede, but it hardly matters what you call it. Suffice it to say that it is one of the most spectacular kites ever to soar into the deep blue sky. However, at the same time it is not a particularly easy kite to fly. You'll need more than a friendly four year old neighbour to get it up into the air.

'The Dragon', as we have decided to call it, is probably used more often as a form of decoration than as a kite to fly. This is a pity, though it would certainly look very elegant on someone's living room wall. But just as bikes are for riding, kites are for flying. They were not really meant to be decorations. So take your dragon outside where it will undoubtedly create quite an impression. It consists of a number of separate kites joined together, and once you have managed to get it up into the air — which requires quite a bit of experience as well as a stiff breeze — you will see that the Dragon really does behave like a dragon. The kite snakes through the air, winding this way and that, attracting a crowd of interested spectators. It inevitably proves to be a first class attraction. Obviously the Dragon is only really attractive if it is appropriately decorated. Use bits of silver or gold foil as well as paint or ink. If the sun's out the Dragon will reflect flashes of light just like the real thing.

The size of the segments: 12 inch in diameter. Each segment is made with a length of cane 1 yard 3.4 inch long and 0.2 inch thick. In addition, you need two pieces of split bamboo 12 inch long. The material used for the kite is silk tissue paper. Make a cross with the lengths of split bamboo and tie them with some cord. Bend the cane into a circle by attaching it to the ends of the cross. Lie the frame on a sheet of paper allowing a hem of about 0.6 inch. Turn over and stick down after making a few cuts. You can make as many segments as you wish, and they are then joined together as shown in the illustration. To decorate the kite, fix two brushes made of dried grasses onto each segment. The Chinese Dragon is especially suitable for painting.

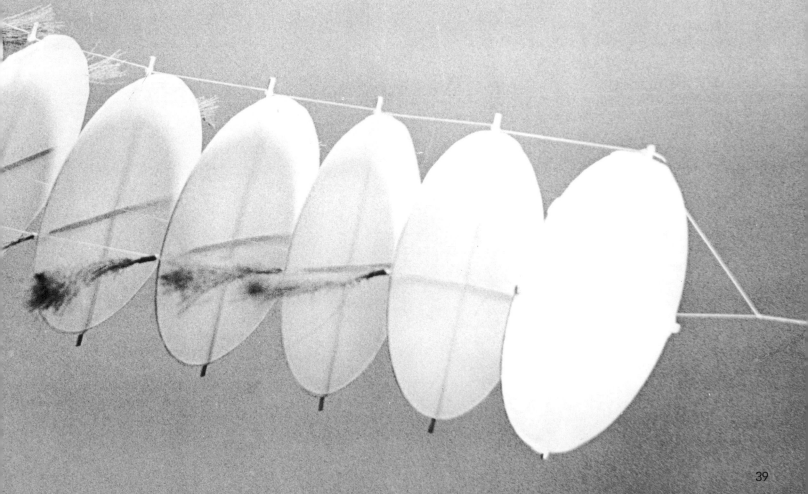

THE THAI SNAKE

When you think about it, the Thai Snake is really a kite made of little more than thin air. The whole point of this kite is its tail, which looks like a snake when it is winding its way through the air in the wind. In fact, the best thing about the Thai Snake is that it will even go up when there's barely a slight breeze blowing.

It was this kite that was used by the King of Siam (present day Thailand) to set a record for flight duration that is almost impossible to break. For two months the Royal Kite flew over the palace to the great satisfaction of His Excellency, though he was hardly holding the string in his own regal fingers. This honour was awarded to the members of his court.

However, these courtiers should certainly not be pitied because the chances are that they were kite lovers. Kite flying is incredibly popular in Thailand. There's even a national kite flying title for winning a competition with seventy-two rules, which is followed with bated breath by the whole country. The champion becomes a national hero overnight.

The Thai snake is not the easiest kite to build, but you can let your imagination run riot. Just think of the Giant Red Cobra or a Blue Spectacled Snake with coloured lenses for eyes. Paper is versatile, and if you want to have more control over your serpent, try flying it on two strings. Even the most coiling snake is easy to steer like this.

Apparently the King of Siam once set a world record for flight duration with this Thai Snake. His Excellency kept the Snake up in the air for two months, though it should never be forgotten that his courtiers held the strings.

Construction.

Really this kite should be made of paper and bamboo, but because the tail is so vulnerable we have chosen wooden dowls for our example. The size of the head is 16 inch tall and 24 inch wide.
It needs three sticks: 0.2 inch thick and 26, 20 and 10 inch long respectively. Bend the 26 inch stick into a curve with a piece of string and attach the bow at right angles to the 20 inch stick. The remaining 10 inch stick is then attached on the bottom of the 20 inch stick. Stretch string over the whole thing (see illustration) and lie the frame on a sheet of paper. Cut the paper in the right pattern allowing 0.6 inch for a hem, but make the hem slightly wider at the top (1.2 inch) as it will not go round the stick otherwise. Hang a tail 9.6 inch wide and as long as you like on the bottom.

To reinforce the tail you can turn over the first piece. You can decorate the kite according to your own taste. It has a two-pointed bridle, as shown in the illustration.
The record length for the tail was set by the kite built and flown by Herman van den Broek and Jan Pieter Kuil. This kite had a tail 700 yard 5 inch long.

Fixing the bridle

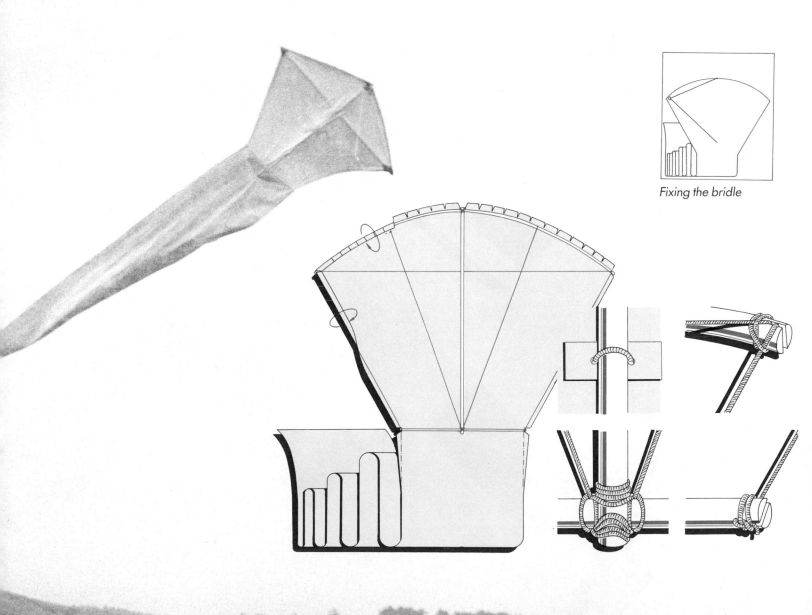

THE HATA

The black sheep in the kite family is undoubtedly the Hata, or more correctly, the Nagasaki Hata, which reveals its place of origin, the port of Nagasaki in Japan. The characteristics of the Hata are that it goes very fast, turns well and is also very easy to fly. It's not surprising that many kite fans rate the Hata as being a better fighter kite than the traditional champion fighter kite from India.

In fact the Hata is apparently descended from the Indian kite, which can clearly be seen from its shape. It's possible that Portuguese and Dutch merchants, who first sailed into Nagasaki in the middle of the sixteenth century, first introduced the Indian fighter kite. Some of the evidence for this idea is that the classic Hata should always be made using the same colours: orange, white and blue — the original colours of the Dutch flag. Moreover, the word 'Hata' actually means flag.

There are many stories about the Nagasaki Hata, all of them quite amazing, and it is very difficult to distinguish between the true stories and total fabrication. During the extremely popular annual kite festival held in Nagasaki in March the story is often repeated how a poor sailor's son, flying his fighter kite, managed to bring down a Hata belonging to an important official on the ship of Emperor Meiji, anchored in Oura Bay. It was not exactly an accident, but Seschichi Obitana, the sailor's son, only realised he had been playing with his own life after committing the evil deed — the kite might have belonged to the Emperor himself, and he was a man who was not particularly renowned for this humanitarian views. Nevertheless, Seschichi was quite petrified when a small boat cast off from the ship with some heavily armed soldiers on board, to ask him his name.

The Hata, or black sheep of the kite family. These illustrations are reproduced from the pattern book of the famous Japanese Nagasaki kite builder, Shigejoshi Morimoto.

Seschichi mumbled his answer and for three weeks suffered agonies of apprehension that at the very least he would end up in prison. Then he received a letter from His Majesty's secretary, complementing him on his wonderful kite and excellent kite flying skill. It goes without saying that Seschichi went on to become one of the most famous kite builders in Nagasaki, and he was succeeded by a long line of others.

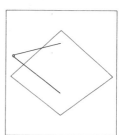

Fixing the bridle

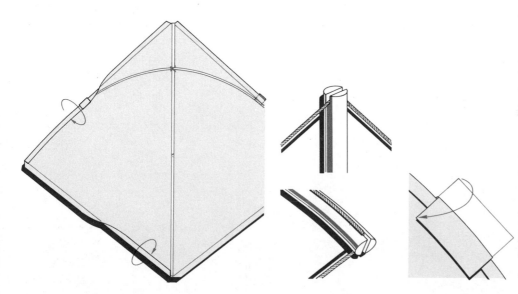

Traditional construction using split bamboo and paper.
Two bamboo sticks are needed for this kite with lengths of 24 and 16 inch respectively. The 24 inch stick should be fixed to the 16 inch stick 2,8 inch from the top end. Stretch string round the whole thing so that the cross-spar is curved (see illustration). Lie the frame on the sheet of paper and cut out the pattern, allowing 0,6 inch for the hem. Where the string and the curved stick meet, the paper should be reinforced with another piece of paper. Attach the bridle as shown in the illustration and reinforce its points with paper.
The kite could be decorated, for example, with your own family shield.

THE KOREAN FIGHTER KITE

The Korean fighter kite is a truly remarkable kite, if only because of the relatively large round hole in the middle of the fabric. Also note the simple rectangular shape and the fins in the right and left corners. The Korean fighter kite is strong, fast, extremely stable, and during a flight it is generally kept under control with a reel.

However, despite its name, the Korean fighter kite is not used in kite battles quite as often as it was in the past. These days it is used much more during the New Year celebrations. On the first day of the New Year the traditional Korean father will chalk the name of a newborn son on a kite (daughters don't seem to have acquired the same status in this ritual) and he then flies the kite. When the kite has gone as high as it can, the father cuts through the string and the kite is left to the mercy of the elements. The purpose of this ritual is to confuse the evil spirits, who see the son's name on the kite and blindly follow it. Obviously the father will be most satisfied if he sees the kite climbing high up in the air and eventually disappearing from sight completely. According to popular belief, all the evil spirits will have gone with the kite, unable to find their way back – even when they realise they have been tricked.

This should serve as a warning to anyone who finds one of these kites lying in his path as he is wandering along. Never pick up a kite. Before you know it, you'll find yourself in all sorts of trouble. It's better to make your own kite.

A few examples of the type of decoration you can use on your Korean fighter kite.

Traditionally the Korean fighter kite is made of tissue paper and bamboo. We have made a kite using transparent kite paper and wooden dowls.
There are five sticks: 2 sticks of 2 feet long, 2 sticks of 4 feet and 1 with the length of 3 feet 4 inches. They are tied together as shown in the illustration and a string is then stretched round the whole thing. Lie the frame on a sheet of paper and cut out the pattern, allowing 0.6 inch for the hem on the sides and bottom, and 1.2 inch at the top. Before turning over and sticking down, cut a hole in the middle of the paper with a 10 inch diameter. (The left over paper can be used for the tail.) Then fold and stick down the hem and make the two tail pieces consisting of 2 elongated triangles of paper stuck onto the corners with glue. The two cross-spars then need to be curved like a bow and finally the bridle is attached. This is a four-pointed bridle. The middle string gives the kite its fighter characteristics.

Fixing the bridle

The Korean fighter kite is particularly striking because of the large round hole in the middle of the fabric.

The Indian fighter kite, ancestor of all the other feared fighter kites which enter into battle into countries such as Korea, Thailand and Japan, and try to outdo each other.

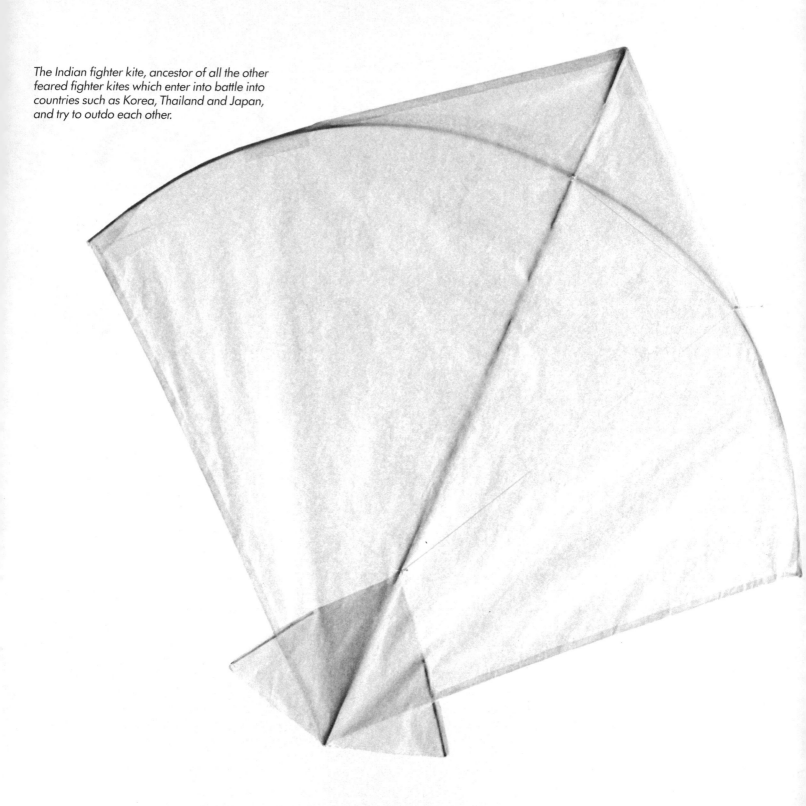

THE INDIAN FIGHTER KITE

The Indian fighter kite is a nasty piece of work. It looks very simple, but watch out, it has a mind of its own. Perhaps this is the reason why it's so popular, the Porsche of kites. It requires a sensitive touch, both for its construction and when you are actually flying it. The Indian fighter kite is not found just anywhere. It is often a bully and has been described as a very self-willed object.

It may look rather plain; flat, no tail, an uninspiring square shape. If you don't keep the string quite taut, it flutters all over the place, and goes anywhere except where you want it to. But when the wind suddenly tugs at it, the Indian fighter kite once again reveals itself to be a rogue, racing through the atmosphere like a rocket.
It can be used to conduct an entire air battle, and these have been held in India for centuries.
The Indian fighter kite is considered to be the mother of all the other notorious fighter kites which battle for supremacy over countries such as Korea, Thailand and Japan. The Hata is one of these descendants – a famous Japanese robber from Nagasaki. The Korean fighter kite with its strange fins is another kite which is descended from its Indian ancestor.

It is therefore a classic kite, and its purpose is purely to lord it over the heavens. It can move as fast as lightning and turn like a slalom skier. A great deal of patience is needed to learn to control it properly, before it will do exactly what you want it to do. But this is the charming side of the rascal. Once you've learned to control it, you couldn't wish for a better kite. Its pedigree is unparalleled.

Construction.
Traditions are meant to be followed, so make the Indian fighter kite in the traditional way from paper and split bamboo. The two bamboo sticks should be respectively 24 and 16 inch long. The 24 inch stick should taper to a point at both ends, and be attached to the 16 inch stick about 2.8 inch from the top. Stretch some thin string around this frame so that the cross-spar is curved (see illustration) and then lie the frame on a sheet of paper. Cut out the pattern allowing 0.6 inch for the hem. It's a good idea to reinforce the construction using some extra paper at the point where the string and the bent cross-spar come together. The tail should be made from two pieces of paper. Stick these pieces on the front and back of the kite with two sticks between them to reinforce it. Attach the bridle as shown in the illustration, and if necessary, reinforce the bridle points with paper.
This kite is an excellent one to decorate with a family coat-of-arms. If your family doesn't have a coat-of-arms, which does sometimes happen, you can always paint your initials on the paper.
Beware of making this kite too large. The Indian fighter kite is meant to be quite small, and in fact people somtimes say: the smaller, the better.

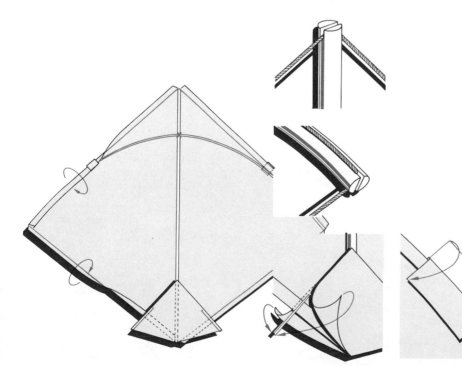

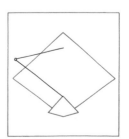

Fixing the bridle

A kite to frighten the living daylights out of anyone – the Suruga.

THE SURUGA

The Suruga is a kite which will frighten the living daylights out of anyone, at least if you paint it with the traditional Japanese patterns. May the fifth is Boys' Day in Japan and during the celebrations all sorts of hideous creatures go up into the sky. It's about time we copied one of their customs, rather than vice-versa. On the other hand, it is not absolutely necessary to paint, for example, a Quasimodo figure on the kite. And I'm not thinking of the Italian Nobel Prize winner for literature but of the charming bell ringer of the Notre Dame who has undoubtedly given palpitations to generations of film buffs with his hideous face. You'd do better to paint the face of your milkman on the kite, the friendly milkman who so generously provided the funds for making the kite. Or you could greet your beloved, who might happen to live a few streets away. This kite has many faces, in true Japanese fashion, particularly when you consider that you could attach two strings, which makes it even easier to steer. You can also put a tail on the Suruga, and this too provides even more scope for the decoration of the kite. For example, it's easy to create a Picasso figure, or try a 1950s pin-up of Brigitte Bardot with her ponytail. The possibilities are endless.

Construction.
Like the Indian fighter kite, the Suruga is also traditionally made of bamboo and paper. For the frame you need three bamboo sticks 36 inch long, and one stick 28 inch long. These sticks are joined together as shown in the illustration, and a fine string is stretched round the frame, after making grooves in the ends of the three sticks.

Take care: as the illustration shows, there are two ways of fixing the string: one runs from the cross-spar, while two strings run straight down from the cross-spar to the two diagonal sticks.

Lie the frame on the paper and cut out the pattern. Don't forget to allow 0.8 inch for a hem on the side where the two pieces of string cross. The paper has to be cut, reinforced with another piece of paper, and stuck down. The sticks of the frame protrude beyond the paper both at the top and the bottom. The four-pointed bridle, the middle section of which increases the fighting capacity, completes the Suruga.

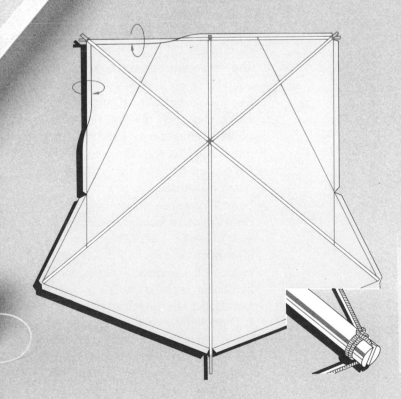

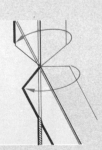

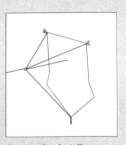

Fixing the bridle

THE SODE

We'll call this kite the Sode kite, although the name isn't absolutely correct. However, it's usually known as the Sode kite.

It's odd that in Japan the Sode kite is nowhere near as popular as, for example, the Hata kite or the possibly even more famous Manbu kite, which depicts the celebrated Japanese legendary figure, Kintoki. Kintoki was raised by bears, and thus became the strongest man in the entire land. The Sode kite is not only a charming object, as its name suggests, but in addition it is simple to make.

Moreover, the Sode kite is very easy to fly and you can perform all sorts of amusing tricks with it. For example, it looks very good when a whole bunch are put together to make one kite. Four or five Sodes, all 39 inch tall, or even twenty-five small ones about 8 inch tall. When these are all joined together, the ensemble provides a fairytale spectacle, especially when all the kites are painted in a special way, each one complementing the next. This demands some thought, both for the painting of the kites and the time at which you let them up — they should always be joined together in the same order, but a real kite fanatic will overcome these problems. It can even provide him with a real challenge, though it doesn't bear thinking about that. Of course, the whole lot could come tumbling down, crashing and tearing to bits in the rhododendrons.

Construction.
A Sode is not the easiest kite to build. Again it is traditionally made of bamboo and paper and these are obviously vulnerable materials. For the frame you need two sticks 24 inch long, one stick 26 inch long and one stick 12 inch long. These are joined together as shown in the illustration.

The whole structure can be reinforced with thin string stretched round the frame. Use the illustration as a guide, then lie the frame on a sheet of paper and cut out the pattern, remembering to allow about 0.8 inch for the hem. Cut away the hem at the corners and stick down the remaining hem and the side.

Something to remember: before sticking down, moisten the paper so that it dries taut. Bridle the kite as shown in the illustration, and the four points can be reinforced with paper if necessary. The kite doesn't need a tail. The Sode is a good kite to fly but is also makes an exceptionally attractive decorative object. You could use the two examples illustrated here as ideas on how to paint your own Sode.

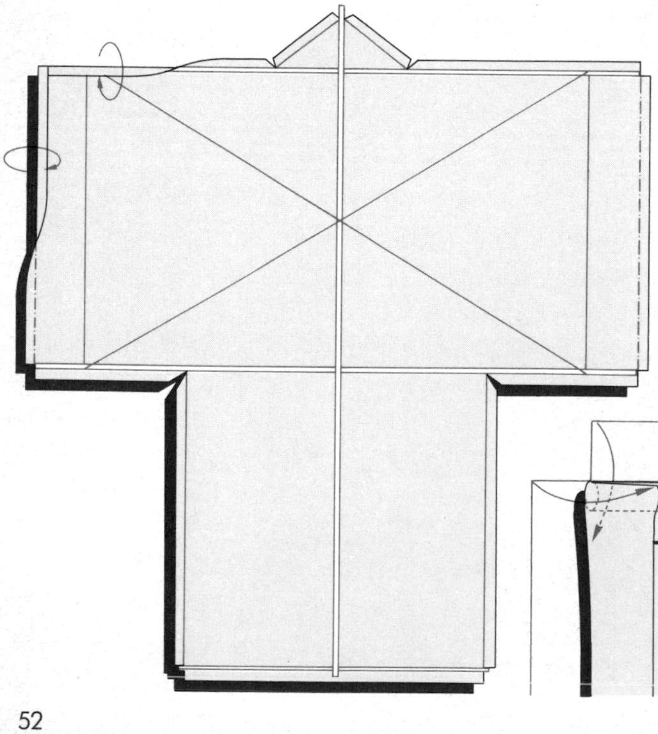

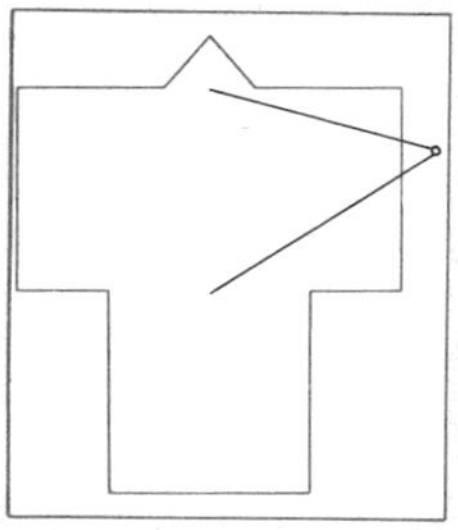

Fixing the bridle.

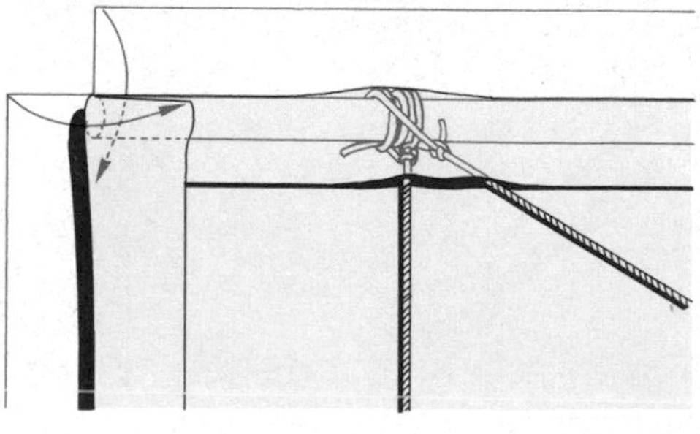

The *Sode* is an excellent kite, and it can be used to perform all manner of tricks.

53

THE HALF MOON

With all due respect, the man who first dreamed up the name 'Half Moon' for this kite, can only be considered half baked from the point of view of modern cretology. In the first place you would need considerable imagination to maintain that the kite even looks like a half moon, and in the second place it never keeps still for a minute.

On the contrary, the Half Moon has a slightly nervous character and likes to dance about. As it probably originated in Hawaii the name 'Hula-hula Kite' might have been more appropriate, particularly as it can be made of bamboo or thin cane instead of fibreglass, which further enhances the South Sea Island effect.

The Half Moon is a kite with all sorts of possibilities. For example, you might consider sending up a number of these round discs one after another. Ten, thirty, even a hundred — as many as you like. It looks even better if the discs are in smaller and smaller sizes from the front to the end of the line. When they're up, get out your Walkman and put on a cassette of Elvis singing 'Blue Hawaii' and you can dream you're lying on the beach at Honolulu.
The Half Moon is a kite with endless possibilities.

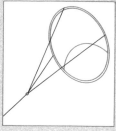

Fixing the bridle

It takes a great deal of skill to fly the Half Moon when there is a stiff breeze.

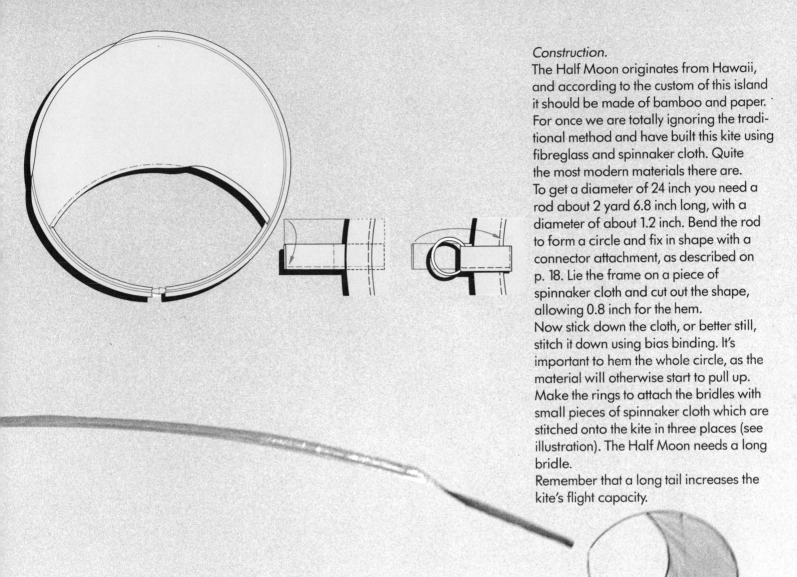

Construction.

The Half Moon originates from Hawaii, and according to the custom of this island it should be made of bamboo and paper. For once we are totally ignoring the traditional method and have built this kite using fibreglass and spinnaker cloth. Quite the most modern materials there are. To get a diameter of 24 inch you need a rod about 2 yard 6.8 inch long, with a diameter of about 1.2 inch. Bend the rod to form a circle and fix in shape with a connector attachment, as described on p. 18. Lie the frame on a piece of spinnaker cloth and cut out the shape, allowing 0.8 inch for the hem.

Now stick down the cloth, or better still, stitch it down using bias binding. It's important to hem the whole circle, as the material will otherwise start to pull up. Make the rings to attach the bridles with small pieces of spinnaker cloth which are stitched onto the kite in three places (see illustration). The Half Moon needs a long bridle.

Remember that a long tail increases the kite's flight capacity.

It doesn't really look like one, but this kite is called the 'Half Moon'.

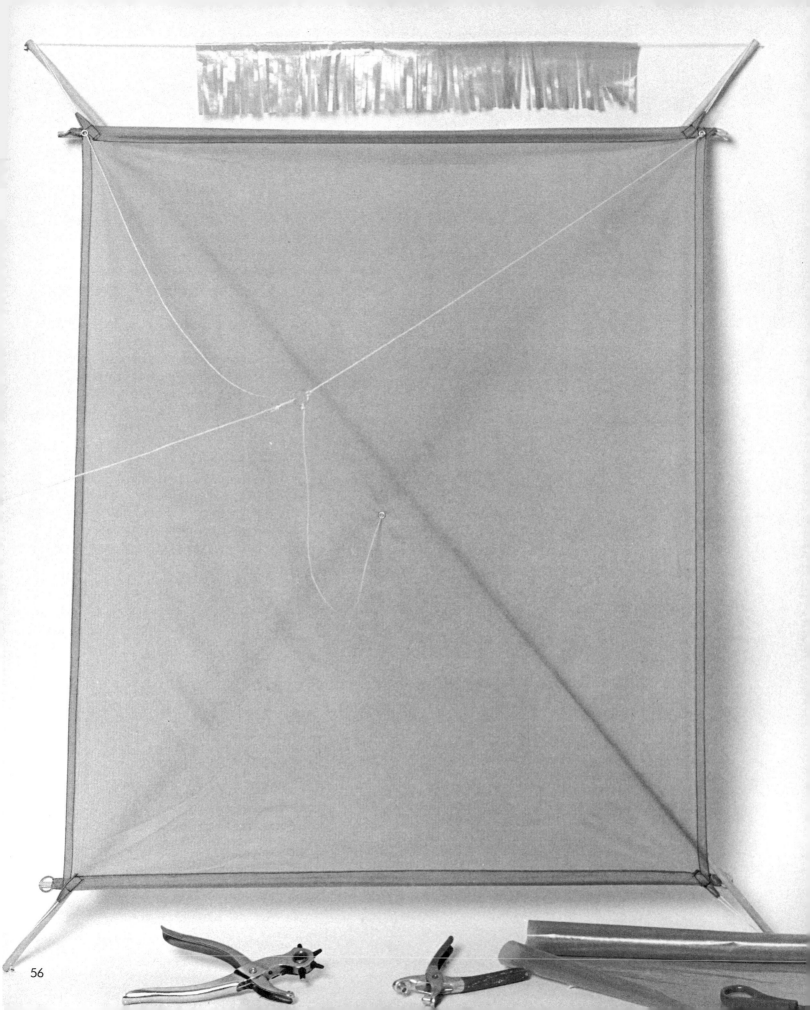

THE RUSSIAN GIANT

This kite is a real giant, though no one knows why it has been called the Russian Giant. And nobody knows whether in the past kite flying was popular on the Russian steppes where there is such a wonderful constant wind. Whatever the reason for it, this kite has always been known as the Russian Giant. In the first place, this must be because it is certainly large – in fact, it's out of all proportion – and secondly perhaps because this kite can make a sound that with a bit of imagination could be compared to the growling of a bear. If you then remember the Russian bear... but as Shakespeare said, 'What's in a name?'

This is an enormous kite but it's easy to make using cheap materials such as bamboo and newspaper. One of the original features is the string, which is stretched between the tops of the crossed bamboo sticks. If you hang strips of paper on this piece of string, they flap in the wind, producing a sound rather like a bear with a speech defect. It's a good way of amusing an angry neighbour just as he's settling down to enjoy the peace of a summer's evening. Be sure to give your Giant a long tail or it might just take a sudden nosedive.

Construction.
This Russian Giant is made of wooden dowls and spinnaker cloth. To make a manageable kite, 40 × 32 inch in size, you will need a piece of spinnaker cloth 44 × 33.6 inch.
Hem this piece of cloth with a 0.4 inch hem, and at the same time stitch a loop on all four corners. These are later used for attaching a ring. Loops also have to be stitched onto the corners for stretching the string through.
Then stitch another hem at the top and bottom, as shown in the illustration. Next take four sticks with a diameter of 0.3 inch. Two of these sticks are 30 inch long and are passed through the hems stitched at the top and bottom of the kite. The sticks of 56 inch are the diagonal sticks. Make a deep groove at the ends of all four sticks and lie the two long sticks on the fabric so that they cross over. They are attached to the fabric with pieces of cord and the four corner loops. The two top ends of the diagonal sticks are tied with a string and the 'buzzer' can be tied onto this string if so desired.
Finally the stick across the top is fixed in such a way that it is slightly curved. The Russian Giant does need a tail, which is also known as 'the loop' (see p. 98). This loop can be given a tassle or normal long tail, hanging down from the middle.
This kite requires a triangular bridle, attached to the two upper corners and the crossover point.

Fixing the bridle

The Russian Giant is very popular with kite enthusiasts who prefer large kites. You can make it as large as you like.

BIRDS AND INSECTS

The butterfly serves as a source of inspiration to kite builders — hardly surprising, in view of its shape. You can paint a kite with the patterns of a butterfly or you can build it in this shape. Similarly, you could also use the shape of a bird as a model to make or to decorate a kite.

Butterfly and bird kites are not even very difficult to build, though at first glance they certainly don't look particularly straightforward. This is often because of the way they have been painted or decorated. A kite shaped like a pheasant looks very complicated when it is silhouetted against the sky, but once you get it down to earth, you will see that the construction is fairly simple. The impressive aspect usually consists of the way in which the wings of the kite have been painted. Why not use your own imagination to make, for example, a double billed cockatoo. There's no such bird, of course, but that's the whole joke of it. Purple, green, yellow, red — any colour can be used, and with a bit of luck and ingenuity you should manage the double bill as well.

It's fairly obvious why kites in the shape of birds or insects are so popular, particularly in China. This is actually where the really fantastic and colourful kites originated, when people discovered how to make paper from rags, in the dim and distant past. Kite flying started off as the preserve of Chinese high society, but from that time onwards the common people started to take up the hobby too, and kites developed by leaps and bounds. The rectangular, rather military-style kite soon made way for all sorts of creations dreamed up by the wonderful Chinese imagination. Even now the Chinese are still amongst the most original kite builders in the world.

Construction.
This bird kite has a span of 6 feet, so it is neither too large nor too small. To make it you will need a piece of spinnaker cloth 40 × 60 inch and two ramin sticks, one 80 inch long with a diameter of 0.2 inch, and one 0.6 inch long with a diameter of 0.2 inch. Cut the sticks in the sizes which you will need, according to the pattern (see illustration). Also cut out the spinnaker cloth in the pattern shown in the illustration, remembering to allow for hems in various places, and for the central seam, which is used to pass the central stick through. Fold the pattern

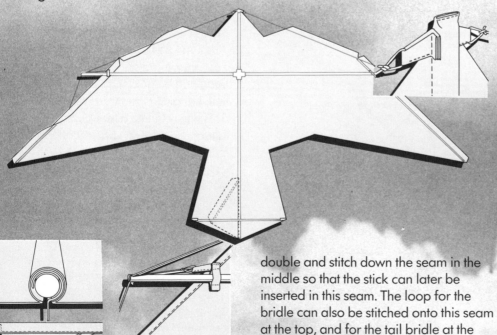

double and stitch down the seam in the middle so that the stick can later be inserted in this seam. The loop for the bridle can also be stitched onto this seam at the top, and for the tail bridle at the tail. You will see how to do this from the illustrations. A narrow hem is now stitched down the wings and 0,2 inch sticks can be inserted in these. A loop is also stitched onto the edges for attaching the string, which is stretched through the grooves at the ends of the crossbars. The

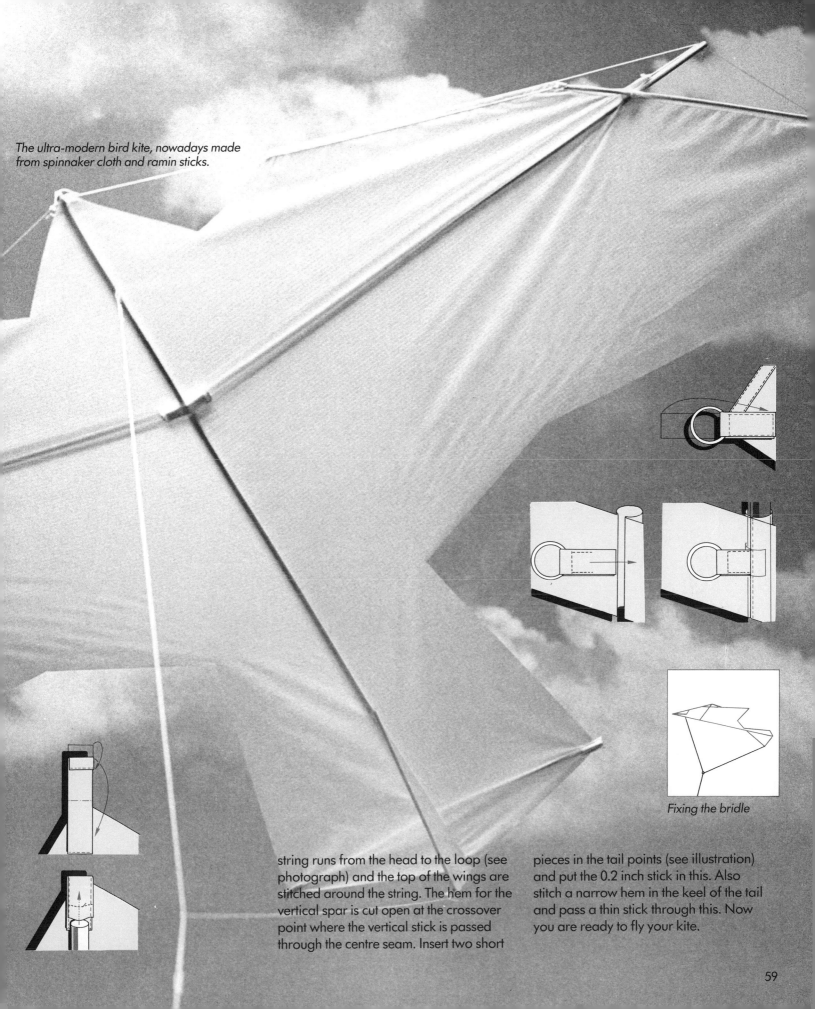

The ultra-modern bird kite, nowadays made from spinnaker cloth and ramin sticks.

Fixing the bridle

string runs from the head to the loop (see photograph) and the top of the wings are stitched around the string. The hem for the vertical spar is cut open at the crossover point where the vertical stick is passed through the centre seam. Insert two short pieces in the tail points (see illustration) and put the 0.2 inch stick in this. Also stitch a narrow hem in the keel of the tail and pass a thin stick through this. Now you are ready to fly your kite.

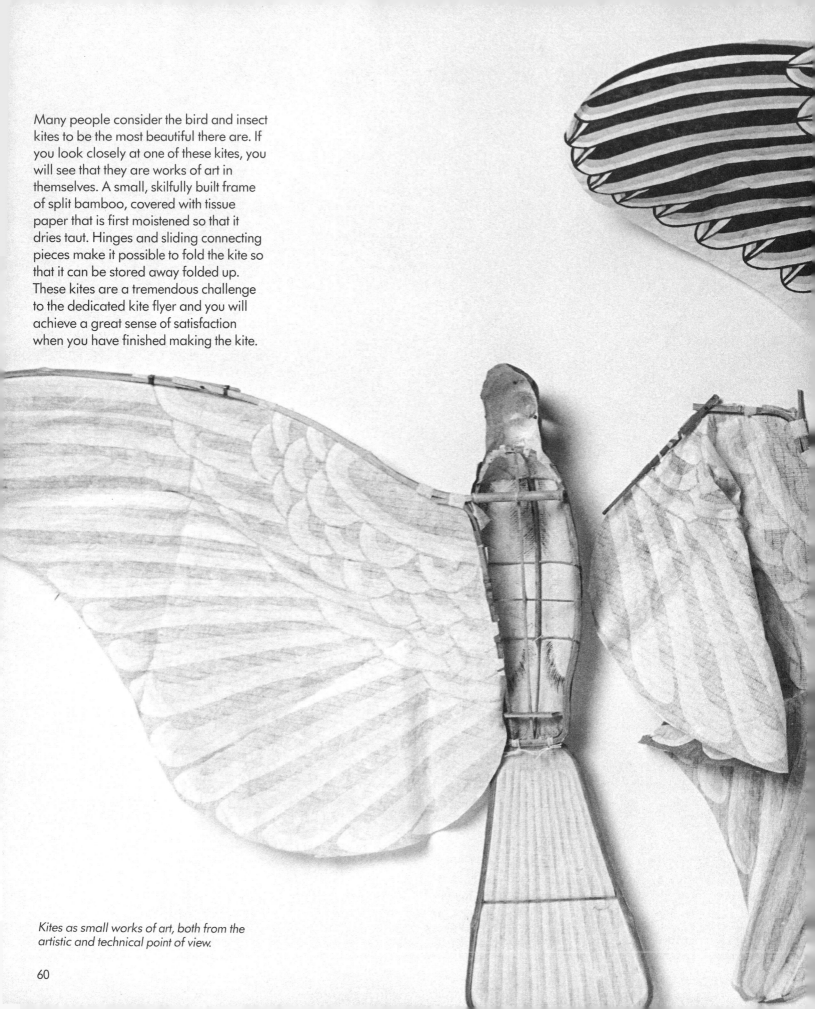

Many people consider the bird and insect kites to be the most beautiful there are. If you look closely at one of these kites, you will see that they are works of art in themselves. A small, skilfully built frame of split bamboo, covered with tissue paper that is first moistened so that it dries taut. Hinges and sliding connecting pieces make it possible to fold the kite so that it can be stored away folded up. These kites are a tremendous challenge to the dedicated kite flyer and you will achieve a great sense of satisfaction when you have finished making the kite.

Kites as small works of art, both from the artistic and technical point of view.

THE DELTA

The ultra-modern kite, the Delta, was designed in 1948 by the American Francis M. Rogallo, though there is some question about whether this kite was the work of a single man. It seems more likely that Rogallo took the last step in completing a design which was first used by rather bold and imaginative inventors in the eleventh century to jump off the tops of church towers, crying:
'I can fly, I can fly'. Severe concussion was probably the very least these pioneers could expect from their exploits, for they knew no more about aerodynamics than a Hungarian farmer knows about submarines. Thus Rogallo is considered to be the father of modern Delta kite flying, although others would claim that Otto Lithenthal deserves this honor. In 1891 this pioneer of aviation wrote the book *Der Vogelflug als Grundlage der Fliegekunst* (Bird flight as a basis for aviation). (It is clear from the title that Lithenthal was a German.) Nowadays his work tends to be ignored, probably because he discovered just three years after the publication of this book, that his 'glider' did not even comply with the safety standards of the time. This discovery came just a little bit too late, and the poor man crashed his contraption in Berlin and died immediately.

This was not to be the fate of Francis M. Rogallo, which makes sense because from the moment that his design was patented, the irreversible trend of delta flying, hang gliding or parasailing got well and truly underway. The sport became extremely popular, especially in the Alps. However, we are not concerned with this new sport here, only with the Delta kite, a kite which will become airborne in the slightest breeze, mainly because of its moveable frame.

This kite is easy to build and easy to fly, and when it's up in the air it looks very good. It's the kind of kite you can sit and watch for hours.

Construction.
The Delta kite is made from spinnaker cloth and wooden dowls of varying lengths. For the particular length required, consult the remainder of the text. If the span of the kite — it can have any span — is chosen to be 80 inch, you need a cloth 60 inch in size. Cut diagonally through the square metre of cloth. Lie the pieces on top of each other and stitch down one short side, at the same time stitching in the keel, which you have placed between the two pieces of cloth (see illustration). When you stitch it double, also make a hem and pass through the centre stick (2 inch in diameter, 39 inch long), hem round the long sides and pass through a stick about 26 inch long and 0.2 inch in diameter. As shown in the illustration, the stick is not passed through the front part of the hem. A third of the way along the stick from the point, attach a connecting piece for the cross-spar. You can attach a ring for passing the string through the keel (see example). The length of the cross-spar is variable.
When there is little wind you will have to use a longer cross-spar than when there is a lot of wind.

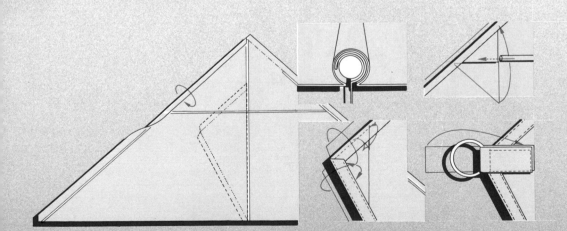

Fixing the bridle

Flying a kite on the beach on a summer evening. Wear your best suit and a collar and tie. Definitely something to remember.

Today's kite — the Delta kite.

BOX KITES

You can never be really sure of these kites — people still argue about who invented the first printing press — but it's generally accepted that the box kite was first invented by Lawrence Hargrave. He first sent up one of these kites in 1893, and as no one could remember ever having seen one before, Hargrave was honoured with the title of inventor.

This is more important than you might suppose at first — for after all, what sort of an invention is a kite — but it was soon discovered in observatories and meteorological stations that as regards reliability there was no kite to equal the one invented by Hargrave. Furthermore, box kites rise up high in the air with tremendous force, which considerably increases the speed at which readings can be taken.

Box kites continued to be used well into the twentieth century, the very same box kites that were almost discovered by accident. Like so many other people, Lawrence Hargrave himself was not so much interested in a reliable kite which could go up quickly, as in an aeroplane which would be capable of taking a person up into the air.

The box kite admittedly took him quite a long way along this path, and once he even made a flight using a number of box kites joined together. These took him up to the dizzying height of five metres, but it was not his fate to discover the aeroplane. He became very disillusioned about this and put an end to his experiments even before the turn of the century, probably not suspecting how important his discoveries had been to aerodynamics in general.

Construction.
Before you start to build this winged box kite, a brief word of warning is in order. You need quite a lot of material for this kite and the material is expensive. On the other hand, the winged box kite is a kite that lasts a long time.

If you wish to make a winged box kite 40 inch high and 16 inch deep and wide, you need two pieces of spinnaker cloth 17 × 65 inch, and four pieces 40 × 16 inch for the wings. The six wooden dowls each have a diameter of 0.3 inch and are 40 inch long. The cells of the box kite should be made from a single piece. The two long sides of the largest piece of spinnaker cloth are hemmed, and then the short sides are stitched together. Cut out the wings as in the pattern shown in the illustration, and hem the long side so that the vertical sticks can be pushed down the hem. Ensure that a piece about 0.8 inch is left open at the top so that the stick will fit into the hem. Then hem around the other two sides. Make an insertion piece on the points of the wings for the cross-spars and stitch the wings onto the cells as shown in the illustrations. The bridles are also as shown in the diagram.

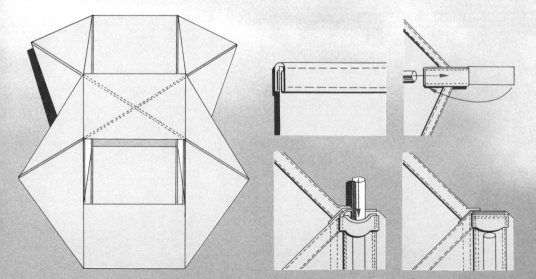

The winged box kite is possibly the most
reliable kite that has ever been constructed.

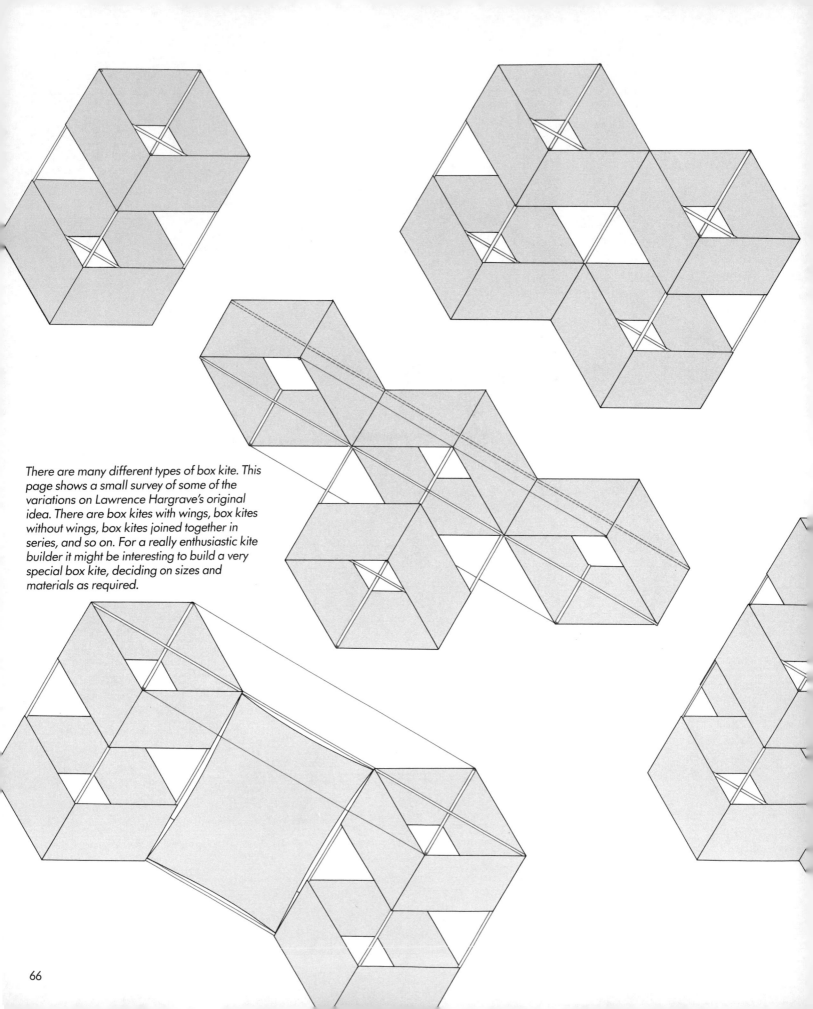

There are many different types of box kite. This page shows a small survey of some of the variations on Lawrence Hargrave's original idea. There are box kites with wings, box kites without wings, box kites joined together in series, and so on. For a really enthusiastic kite builder it might be interesting to build a very special box kite, deciding on sizes and materials as required.

THE MULTIPLE

Flying B2 blocks, painted all sorts of colours? You could almost believe in them if you didn't know any better. But of course, the real kite expert does know more about these things, and will recognize these creations for what they are — a number of box kites joined together and known as a 'multiple'.

Anyone at the 1984 kite festival in Scheveningen will be aware of the endless possibilities of these box kites. You can use them in all sorts of different ways, small ones, large ones, one behind the other, one on top of another. No matter how you arrange them, they will fly, as the early pioneers using box kites, such as Hargrave, Bell, Cody and Saul discovered decades ago.

The things box kites have been used for! They've been sent up carrying advertisements on banners, they've taken people up into the air, they were used during the Second World War to harass aeroplanes, and, last but by no means least, they were made just for fun.

Like father, like son. Putting together a flying B2 block (or 'Multiple', as this kite is officially known) at the 1984 kite festival in Scheveningen (see left).

The multiple just keeps on flying.

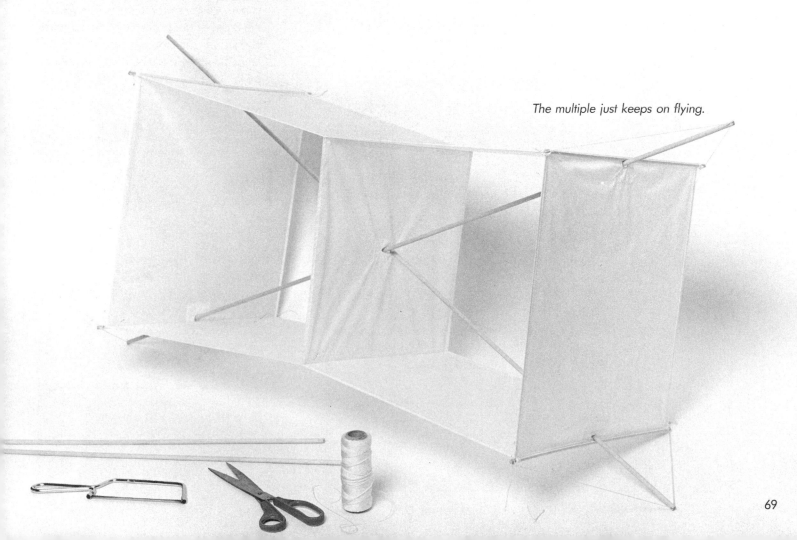

This is what Walter Brook made box kites for. He made such amusing and entertaining models that even the English court became interested. Walter Brook was invited to design a few kites for the palace, and this posed no problems for the ingenious Mr. Brook. He also received orders for ministers who took up the hobby. It did not take long for 'Brookite' to develop into an entire kite industry which exists to this very day and supplies kites throughout the world.

Thus it's possible to buy à box kite (from Brookite or other manufacturers), but it's also possible to make your own if you happen to be short of cash. It may look rather complicated, but appearances are deceptive. If you don't believe it, just have a go.

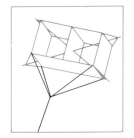

Fixing the bridle

Construction.

If you have four sticks 16 inch long, two sticks 47 inch long (with a diameter of 0.3 inch), one piece of spinnaker cloth 18 × 18 inch and one piece of spinnaker cloth of 100 × 18 inch, you can make a multiple cell of 32 × 16 × 16 inch, and that is really quite large. Nevertheless, it will soar into the air like a bird, because that's the Multiple's great strength. Hem round the long sides of the large piece of cloth and stitch the short sides together. Then stitch a seam down the four corners and pass the sticks down these seams. Hem round all four sides of the middle piece (the cloth 18 × 18 inch) and attach it to the middle of the long side of the cell as shown in the illustration. Now reinforce the middle of this piece as shown. Also reinforce the points where the cross-spars protrude at the corners. The strings run through a groove that you have cut in the ends of the cross-spars at all the corners.

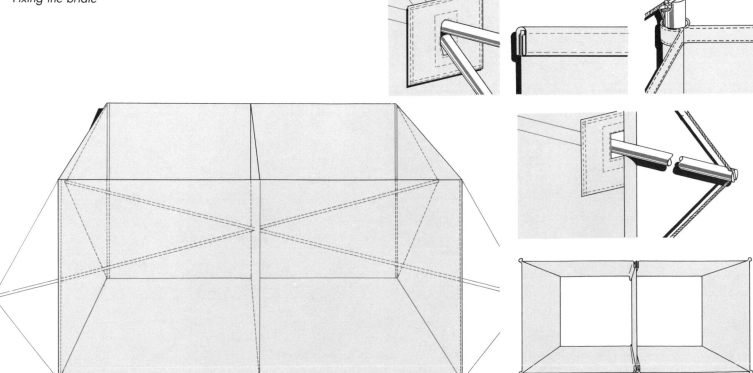

For real enthusiasts: the sticks which have been put in the corner points make it possible to join cells together. If you use longer sticks to do this – these should also be thicker – it is possible to slide other cells over them. It's also possible to make a whole train of cells which are joined together with string but are nevertheless very flexible.

This sort of kite can be endlessly extended, with spectacular results, both lengthways and widthways.

Using the 'Multiple' as a basis you can build a kite which cannot be bettered. However, we will give you a few ideas to get you going.

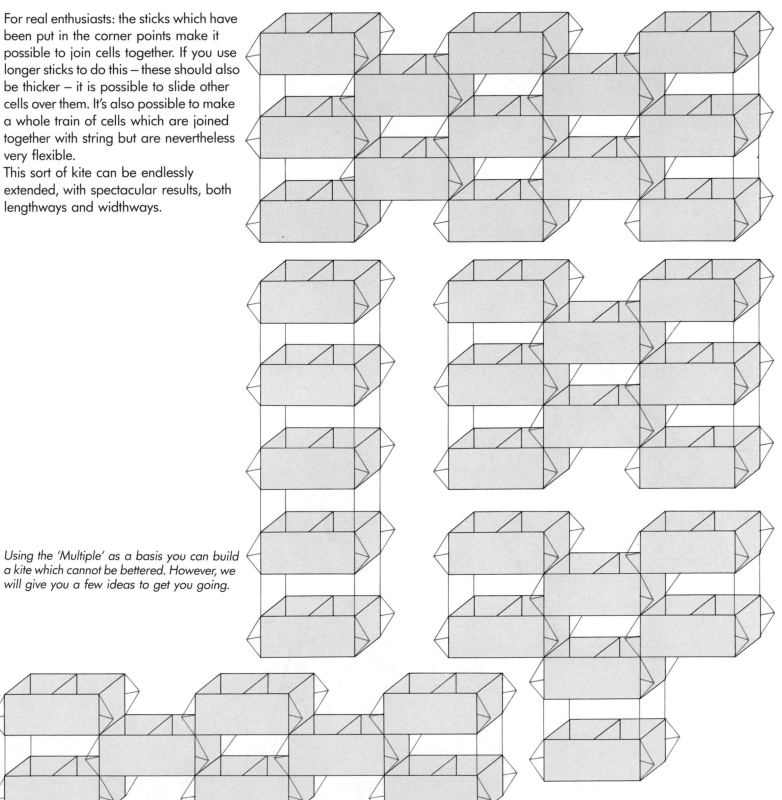

FACET

The Facet appeared out of nowhere from one day to the next. No one knows who invented it or where it first went up into the sky, but probably it was 'invented' by scores of people throughout the world at the same time. This kite looks terribly complicated but there are people who can put it together in half an hour. The Facet is composed of squares, though it looks like a crystal of triangles.

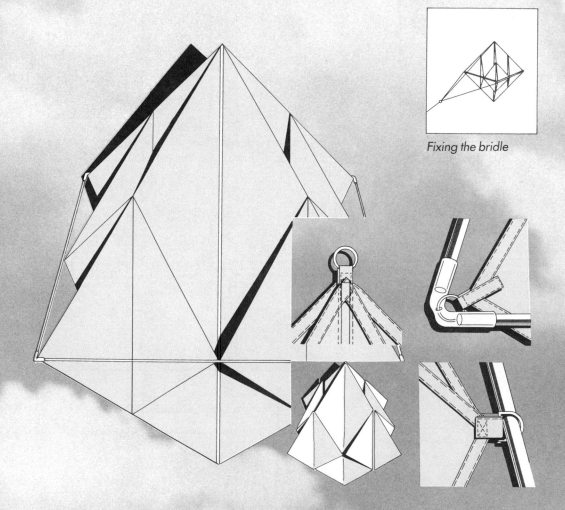

Fixing the bridle

The Facet is for sale in every kite shop but it is also an extremely interesting model to make yourself.

Construction.

For this Facet you will need two pieces of spinnaker cloth 24 × 24 inch, four pieces 12 × 12 inch, four sticks 24 inch long with a diameter of 0.2 inch, one stick 32 inch long with a diameter of 0.3 inch, four pieces of PVC tubing 2 inch long, and ten keyrings. This sounds rather complicated, but anyone who is put off by this list of components may rest assured that the kite is fairly simple to make.

The two large pieces of cloth are hemmed round all sides with a hem 0.4 inch wide and then laid one on top of the other. Stitch them together along the diagonal with a seam in the middle, and pass the 32 inch stick through this seam. The four small squares are also hemmed and laid down on the points of the large squares.

Now stitch these pieces along the diagonal as shown in the example. Loops made of spinnaker cloth are sewn onto the four outer corners. Put the rings through these loops, pricking them through the pieces of PVC tubing. Turn over the other ends of the triangles and stitch them together in pairs. Again, see the illustration.

Stitch a strip of cloth with a ring onto the seam where the triangles are joined together. Finally stitch a strip of cloth with a ring onto both points of the kite — this can serve as a bridle on tail point. Pass the sticks through the rings and in the PVC tubing, attach the bridle and you are ready to fly the kite. There's no need for a tail.

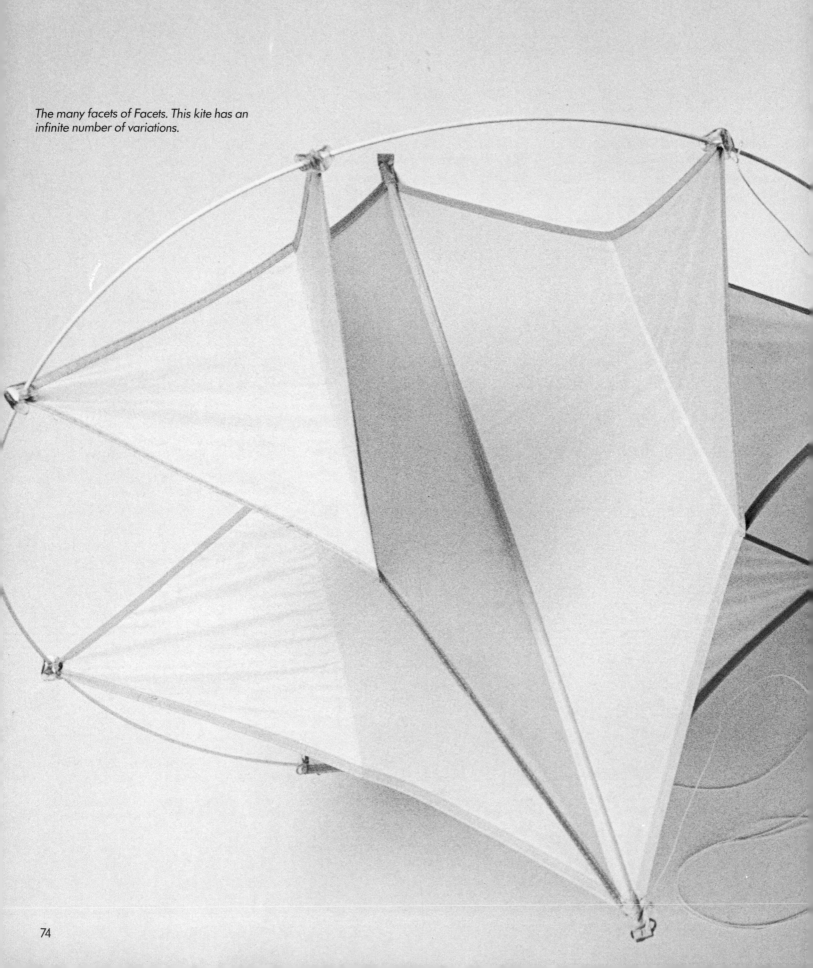

The many facets of Facets. This kite has an infinite number of variations.

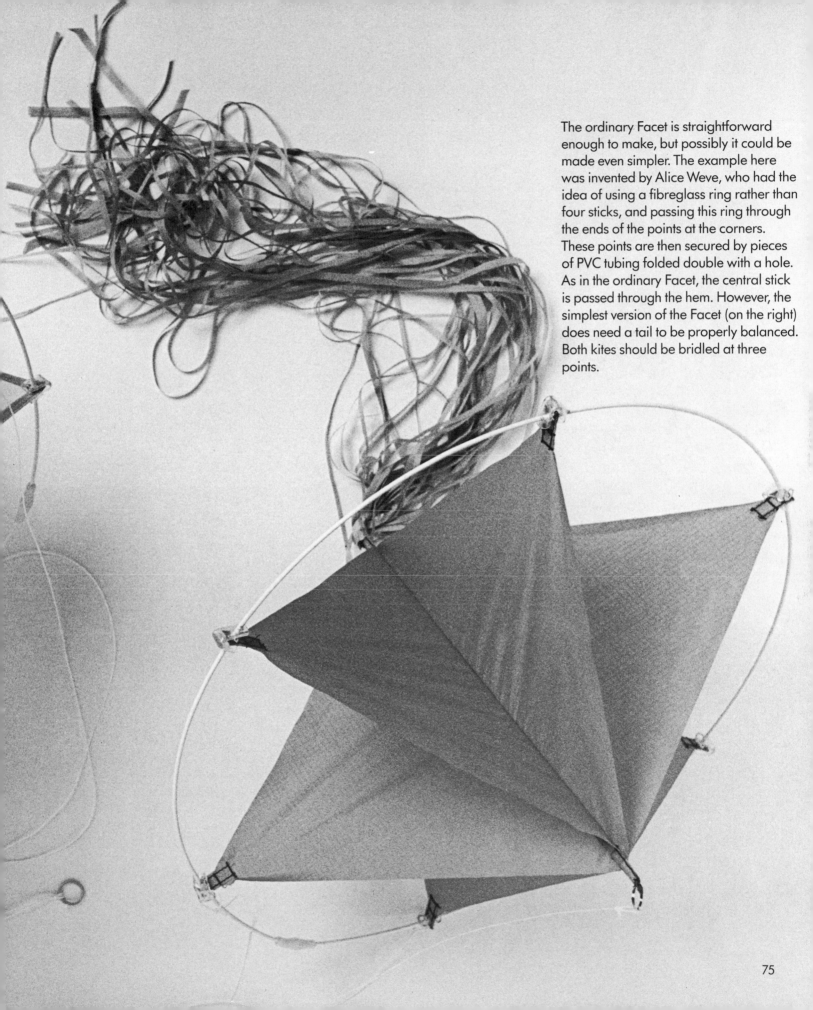

The ordinary Facet is straightforward enough to make, but possibly it could be made even simpler. The example here was invented by Alice Weve, who had the idea of using a fibreglass ring rather than four sticks, and passing this ring through the ends of the points at the corners. These points are then secured by pieces of PVC tubing folded double with a hole. As in the ordinary Facet, the central stick is passed through the hem. However, the simplest version of the Facet (on the right) does need a tail to be properly balanced. Both kites should be bridled at three points.

TETRA (NICK MORSE)

The kites of Dr Alexander Graham Bell, the inventor of the telephone, had one disadvantage: the frame consisted of innumerable sticks and rods so that the tetrahedron (structure) was often rather heavy. However, this learned man's kites were certainly stable and it cannot be denied that they were quite strong. Once, one of these tetrahedrons took one of Bell's assistants almost ten metres up into the air. The poor fellow was almost shocked out of his wits, but fortunately had the presence of mind to hold tight.

Later on Bell's kites achieved even more startling results though his successes were rather eclipsed with the development of aviation. They were ungainly and difficult to build for people who saw kite flying as a hobby rather than a science. However, not all that long ago, a certain Nick Morse had a wonderful brainwave. Morse invented a type of umbrella construction which meant that Bell's 'tetra', the abbreviation of its rather complicated name, could be folded open. Moreover, he did not use six sticks per cell, in the normal way, but four. These four sticks were of the lightest possible material. They join together in a PVC connecting piece, and are also connected at the other ends.

Even Alexander Graham Bell would have been delighted with the result, if he had lived to see it. The possibilities of the Tetra are infinite. By using special fabrics and fixing the strings in a particular way, the kite has a unique shape. The tetra's pre-war strength and durability has been transformed into a modern version.

Construction.

A tetra kite is built like an umbrella. The dimensions can vary, but for this one, which has cells 16 × 16 inch, you need a stick 5.5 yard long with a diameter of 0.19 inch. You also need over one square yard.

of cloth which is cut into eight triangles with two sides of 16 inch each. These triangles are necessary because the grain of the fabric is important when the cloth is pulled taut. Every cell is held by four sticks which meet at a cross piece made of two pieces of PVC tubing tacked together. One side (see example) has a hole so that it is easier to mount the cloth. The corners are joined together with rubber tubing and rings. The strings in the cell keep the whole thing in shape. The inventor of this unique contraption was an Englishman, Nick Morse. You can see yourself how easy this Tetra kite is to fly, using a three point bridle.

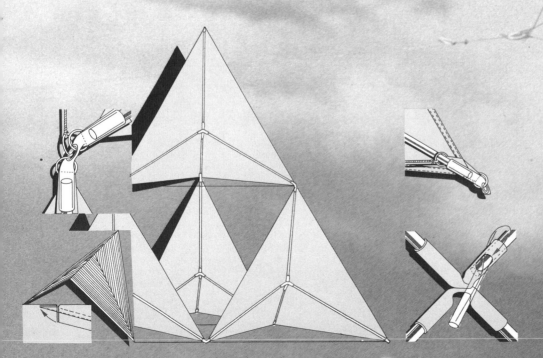

Fixing the bridle

The Tetra kite: a modern version of a solid pre-war model.

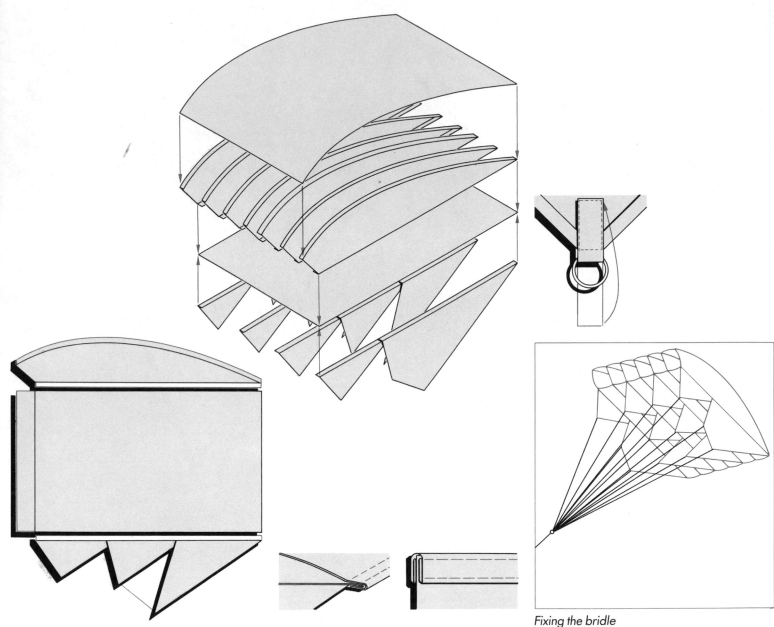

Fixing the bridle

Construction.

Be warned before you start, the Parafoil is complicated and, moreover, an expensive kite to build. It's really a job for a professional, and it's important to follow the instructions and the illustrations very carefully.

We have chosen to build a kite of 60 × 80 inch, and for this size you will need two pieces of spinnaker cloth of 64 × 84 inch, one piece of 84 × 80 inch, one piece of 84 × 80 inch (for the ribs) and one piece of 80 × 40 inch (for the keels). Obviously, sticks are not required. The whole thing is cut to size (see example) and stapled together with a stapler. It has to be stapled first to prevent the various parts from sliding when they are stitched together. (In fact, it is often advisable to use a stapler before stitching when you are making some of the other kites described in this book.)

To strengthen the kite, hem round the front of the ribs, the top and bottom decks and all the sides of the keels. Stitch down the back of the air cells.

If you use different bright colours, your Parafoil will look really beautiful. It's no easy matter to attach the bridle to this 'flying airbed'. You'll soon realize that the Parafoil should be rather 'hollow' to fix the bridle, but even then you may encounter difficulties. This is a difficult kite to make, but possibly all the more fascinating for that reason.

PARAFOIL

Can a parafoil really be considered a kite — or is it actually more of a parachute, or even a glider? Perhaps you think you know. All we can say is that it was originally developed by Domina C. Jalbert, who also called it his 'flying mattress'.

He developed it rather than invented it, for he worked on his idea for twenty or thirty years and kept on incorporating parts of other people's ideas into his own. Jalbert started more or less by copying the wings of his sports plane, using canvas on the frame instead of aluminium.
The results far exceeded Jalbert's expectations, especially with regard to the force with which his flying mattress rose up in the air. He carried out more experiments and adapted his original model with additional flaps attached to the bottom of the mattress (to retain the air more effectively), and also added a valve system which allows you to let out this air when required.

The potential uses of the parafoil increased every time he thought of something new, and the end result is that it's now used for all sorts of purposes. The best known — or, at any rate, the most spectacular use — is undoubtedly its application as a parachute with steering. Nowadays you will often see the heroes tumbling out of a plane on one of these dirigible parachutes to land on a previously determined spot, as close as possible to the spectators; for example, at an important football match, when a sports complex is opened, or at a children's gala.
In nine out of ten cases the parachutists actually succeed in landing in the right spot, which shows what fun it is to fly in one of these parafoils.

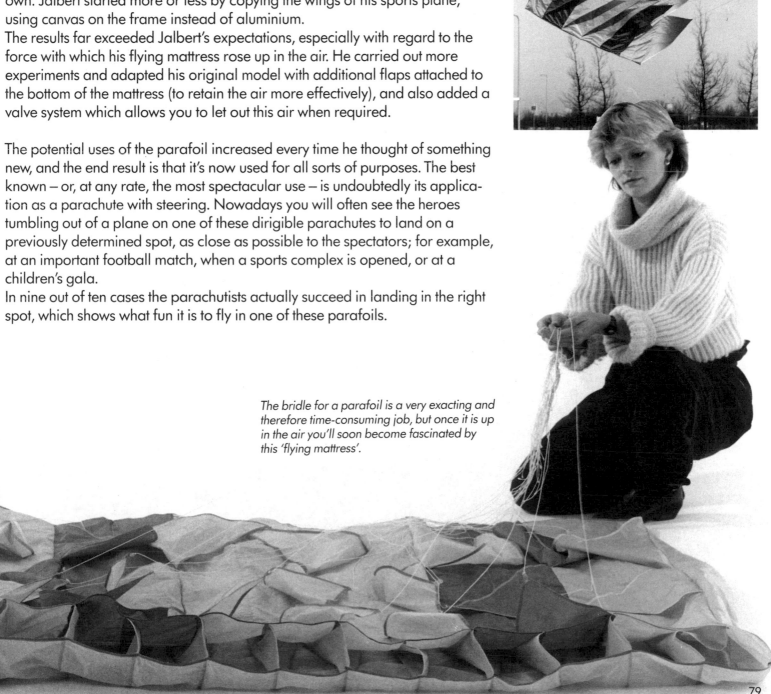

The bridle for a parafoil is a very exacting and therefore time-consuming job, but once it is up in the air you'll soon become fascinated by this 'flying mattress'.

THE SLED SPECIAL

The Sled Special is a sled kite according to the principle of the parafoil described earlier in this book. Nick Morse first thought of constructing one of these kites, and if you really want to make an impression in the local park one Sunday morning, try strolling up with one of these under your arm.

Morse's idea was as simple as it was effective. Take the sticks out of the sled kite and replace them with a few air passages like those in the parafoil. If the reader has read through the chapter on parafoils he will understand what happens: the air currents make the Sled Special go rigid at the same time as providing it with a lift.

You can make the Sled Special into a really fantastic kite, a kite quite unlike any other for miles around.
In addition, this kite is absolutely unaffected by high winds or a total lack of wind. It is advisable to adjust the bridle of an orthodox kite to the force of the wind, but for Morse's Sled Special this is quite unnecessary. It is fully automatic and automatically adapts to any weather conditions. We are all indebted to Nick Morse.

Construction.
The Sled Special – another great invention by the English kite fanatic, Nick Morse. This kite could be considered as a sophisticated combination of a parafoil and sled kite and it can be built in any size.
To make the kite shown here, you need a piece of spinnaker cloth 39 × 28 inch in size. It is hemmed all the way round with a length of tape to make it look more attractive, but obviously this is not absolutely necessary. This kite can be made very largely according to the builder's own taste and preference.
Cut out the pattern from the spinnaker cloth as shown in the illustration. Hem round, and if desired, stitch round the hem with tape. The Sled Special's 'engines', or two air tunnels, are made using the method illustrated in the example. Make two holes in the keels of the kite with a hole punch, and attach the bridle to this.
The Sled Special is one of the kites which is especially suitable for making a train. Twenty of these kites could be joined together. It might be rather difficult to get them all up in the air together, but once it's flying through the sky people will stop and stare at this spectacle with mouths agape.

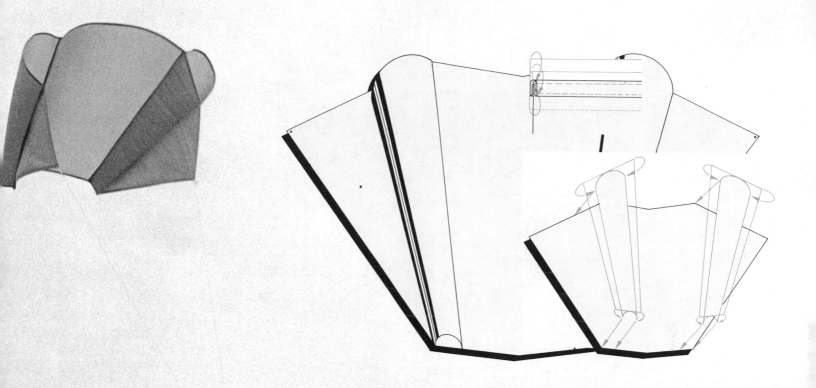

Fixing the bridle

If you really want to make an impression in your local park, think about building one of these Sled Specials.

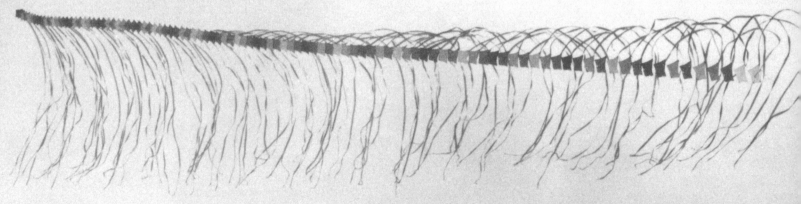

THE STUNT KITE

If it weren't for the fact that you can see the string, you'd think that these kites are controlled by remote control. The Stunt Kite is a kite which certainly never becomes boring. It's a nervous sprinter and when the wind is up it can chase through the sky at 70 m.p.h. It's quite unpredictable and can give spectators the fright of their lives by suddenly hurtling towards the ground. At the same time it's a prima donna when you fly it in a chorus line of similar kites in a well choreographed ensemble against the blue sky.

This kite has a steering mechanism which was originally the idea of Peter Powell, who made a breakthrough in kite flying some time ago with his revolutionary 'stunter'. No kite had ever been built before which was so easy to steer with just a few small tugs on the strings. With one tug on the right the stunter swoops to the right; one tug on the left and it races back in the opposite direction.

It's a pure thoroughbred – which also means that at first it's best to have some assistance from someone who's had experience with this type of kite, if only to get it up into the air. One uncontrolled movement and the kite may do a nose-dive into the grass, and as we all know, kites are not made of concrete.

Joining a number of these Stunters together is very effective. At the kite festival in Scheveningen in 1984, one hundred stunters were tied together and then let up, pulled by a jeep, providing a sensational spectacle. The 'ohs' and 'ahs' of appreciation became all the more strong when all the kites looped the loop. But the best thing of all is that the stunt kite is on sale everywhere, and it's also quite easy to build yourself.

A sensational spectacle at the kite festival in Scheveningen in 1984. A hundred stunt kites tied together doing a loop the loop, and causing gasps of delight everywhere. Actually, this stunt with stunt kites is not one for amateurs to try.
At Scheveningen two experienced kite flyers were at the wheel, a steering rod on a jeep. Obviously it would never have been possible to do the stunt by hand, and certainly not a hundred at the same time, beautifully arranged according to colour, with tails about ten metres long. What can the breaking strain of these kites have been? Possibly two thousand lbs?

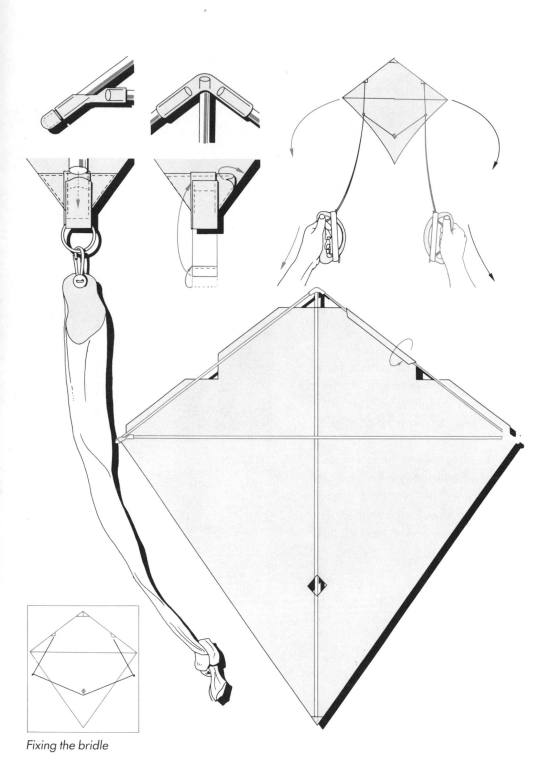

Fixing the bridle

This illustration clearly shows the various parts of this version of the Stunt kite.

Construction.

Peter Powell's Stunt Kite is on sale in every kite shop. After all, it is a thoroughbred. But because this book was written for do-it-yourself enthusiasts, people who like making their own kites, a description follows below of how to build one of these popular stunt kites, based on an original design. Because the kite can be flown both in a strong wind and when there's very little wind, it's best to make it from fibreglass rods and polythene. Obviously Spinnaker cloth can also be used. Cut out the fabric according to the pattern, though changing this pattern slightly will not be fatal. In fact, the stunt kite could even be made in a diamond shape. The top point should be made from a piece of 'protected' tubing (with a hole in the middle) which holds together the three rods (in this case 20 inch for the side pieces and 28 inch for the vertical spar).

The cross-spar is attached to the side pieces using a short length of rubber tubing cut for this purpose. Secure the tubing with a rubber cap which is glued onto the end of the rod. Glue or stick the fabric around the side pieces, and reinforce the point at the bottom with a triangle of fabric, gluing or stitching down. It's a good idea to put a ring on the connecting piece so that the tail can be attached to this with a clip.

Cut out the fabric where the bridle will be attached and affix the bridles onto the sticks with tape. Make a double bridle or it won't be possible to steer the kite. The tail is made from a piece of polythene tubing (which is widely used in the packaging industry), and is knotted at the end.

N.b. The cross in the middle of the kite should not be fixed because of the force exerted on the kite by the wind etc. Another advantage of having a cross which is not fixed is that this makes the stunt kite easy to take apart.

Finally, don't panic when you're flying it. The stunt kite will react to the slightest tug on the string – so keep cool.

An elegant dance executed by two stunt kites joined together.

One of the many experiments carried out by the British Navy with one of the kites developed by Cody at the beginning of the century.

CODY

Samuel Franklin Cody's name will no longer be familiar to the general public, and even most kite enthusiasts will be at a loss if asked who he was. Nevertheless, this Texas born kite flyer was an enthusiast of exceptional calibre. It's a pity that the poor man suffered from an unfortunate past, which meant that he was often considered with some suspicion.

In 1861 Cody was born in Birdville, Texas, and if his biography (*Pioneer of the Air* by G.A. Broomfield) is to be believed, there was no one in the still very wild Wild West of the United States of America who was quite as handy with a Winchester or a lasso. A latter day Wyatt Earp, the man who could shoot faster than his shadow.

However, Cody soon realized that he would never make his fortune going round herding up buffalo, so he made his way to the Klondyke and the Yukon, where gold was said to be lying around for the taking. These reports proved to be exaggerated, and no matter how long Cody went on panning and digging for gold, he found nothing. As the history books reveal, he was by no means the only one.

The alternative seemed to be to return to buffalo hunting, but Cody had a better offer. He travelled around America with a circus, and became extremely successful. He was billed as the King of the Cowboys, and in fact he really looked just like a cowboy, galloping through the arena, swinging his lasso. The spectators were so impressed with all his skill and fine tricks that the circus director cried buckets when Cody decided to go to England, and that was the end of his finest attraction.

Samuel Franklin Cody as he liked to be portrayed – rather like Buffalo Bill.

However, Cody knew what he wanted. He had seen the legendary Buffalo Bill himself doing his show, and because he considered – probably rightly – that he could do whatever Buffalo Bill could, he worked on the assumption that a similar Wild West show would be a great success in England.

It soon transpired that he had been quite right. The English couldn't get enough of this man with his long hair, pointed beard, enormous moustache, stetson, wide leather belt, slim hips and beautifully tooled cowboy boots. So this is what the Wild West was all about. The harder the whips cracked, the louder the horses snorted, the better they liked it. Every time Samuel Franklin Cody saved a beautiful young lady tied to a totem pole from a certain grisly death at the very last moment, the rows on rows of spectators would heave a sigh of relief.

Admittedly the 'Klondyke Nugget', as the show was called, relied very little on Shakespearian drama – or, to put it bluntly – it was a pretty common show.

Mr Cody in his ordinary clothes.

Nevertheless, Cody was quite a character, with a lasso in his right hand as another two unfortunates bit the dust, the first of five dozen or so. Cody seemed to be invincible.

However, just imagine what it must be like dispatching all these instant villains (either to the hereafter or to cool off) during the matinee performance, only to find that you had to do the same job again in exactly the same way in the evening, night after night. It gets rather tedious, especially when you find that the rabble you thought you'd finished off in the afternoon are ready to start all over again in the evening.

Cody began to look for other challenges and discovered the hobby of his son, Leon, who had become addicted to flying kites. Cody wondered whether it wouldn't be possible to get a man in the air using this method. He started work on this project straightaway, and his experiments very soon produced results. Cody turned out to be a born kite builder – after all, he originally hailed from Birdville – and by 1901 he had successfully managed to leave terra firma with a kite, watched by representatives from the British Ministry of Defence. This was another proof of the showmanship of the King of the Cowboys. That's how his achievements were viewed by the general public, but Cody was convinced that his kite – or rather his system of kites – was extremely suitable for use as an observation post, for example, for military reconnaisance. The man flying in the kite, equipped with binoculars, a camera, a gun, and possibly even a telephone, could be invaluable in combatting the enemy. For this reason he continued pestering the Ministry with increasingly improved versions of his kite.

Perhaps this was why they were not particularly impressed by all the brainwaves of this former showman. On the other hand, they certainly had enormous respect for the American's marksmanship. He was invited to become a shooting instructor at the military academy in Aldershot. However, Cody wasn't at all interested in this proposal; he found kite flying a far more attractive pastime.

He began to do stunts. He even dared to attempt to cross the English Channel from Calais to Dover in November 1903 to prove the strength of his increasingly large contraptions. He made his attempt in a sloop, to prevent any misunderstandings, but this sloop was pulled along by a Cody kite. Cody actually managed to reach the French shore without getting his feet wet, and the publicity he gained from this enterprise finally caused the military authorities to sit up and take notice. The time was considered ripe to reach some agreement with this intrepid kite builder. Suddenly the sky was the limit. He merely had to snap his fingers when he wanted a few warships to carry out tests with his kites, and the ships would appear as if by magic.

The Royal Marines were particularly impressed with the results of his tests.

One of the first Cody kites, held by the grand master himself (right) and an assistant. Cody had attached wings to the box kite originally designed by Hargrave.

Cody on his famous white stallion inspecting his kite squadron in about 1905.

Once a soldier named Moreton, who hadn't flinched in the trenches and obviously didn't know the meaning of fear, had gone up a good 800 metres with one of these Cody kites.

This clinched the matter. Cody was immediately promoted to the rank of an officer in the British Army and was appointed Chief Kite Instructor. He was supposed to be occupied with designing and building even better kites, as well as supervising the training of up and coming kite flyers. Samuel Franklin Cody was where he wanted to be.

By this time the fee he was earning for pursuing his hobby was a thousand pounds – no mean sum in those days – and kites had in fact become his profession. Furthermore, no one seemed to mind when he mounted his favorite white steed to go for a ride and take a break from sawing, sticking and gluing. He was keen on building kites, but horse riding was his real passion, even when, after a while, he switched from building kites to building aeroplanes.

This was to be Cody's downfall. When he realized that his 'war kites' had been leading him on the wrong path he immediately changed to building aeroplanes. He was no fool, and eventually became the first man in England not only to build his own motorized aircraft, but also to fly this contraption himself. However, motorized aircraft, seems rather an ambitious description. When you see the photographs of the historic moment, it is difficult to deny the fact that Cody's invention hardly deserves the name of aeroplane. It would be more correct to call it an engine powered kite.

Cody is no longer alive but his spirit lives on.
This photograph of Pete Pronk was made in
Bath in 1981. Unfortunately it is not known how
high he managed to fly up into the air with this
Cody kite.

This kite (right), built by Cody in 1908, gained him enormous admiration. It was the strongest and most reliable kite of the time and carried quite a number of daredevils high up into the sky.

Displaying a Cody kite. The construction of this kite is described on the following pages. From left to right: Alice Weve, who advised on the models in this book, and built them; David Van Dijk, photographer, and Jack Botermans (lay-out). The two drawings are of the author, Rob van den Dobbelsteen (above) and the illustrator, Toon van der Struijck (under).

92

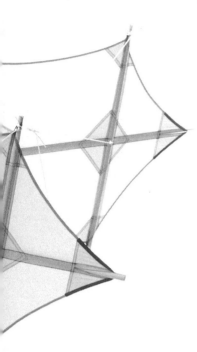

A man whose name can be found repeatedly in this book, Nick Morse, in action. Morse can be considered as one of the trendsetters in the world of kites. Kites are more than a hobby for him – they have become his profession. This picture shows him standing in a basket inside a Cody lift kite which he built himself. Morse also made a Malay train with kites 13 feet high. Bell's tetra kites were also very popular with this Englishman.

Cody soon found this himself and it was not long before he produced designs which looked more like real aeroplanes. There's a famous photograph in which he can be seen at the wheel of a warplane he constructed in 1909 in Aldershot. Little was left of the former cowboy. He was now a real aviator, complete with R.A.F. moustache in the true Biggles tradition.

Four years later he was killed in Aldershot, or to be precise, in the sky above the base. A sudden gust of wind ripped apart the 'Waterplane' which he had built himself. The passenger in the other seat also died in the crash.
The American daredevil pilot was not only mourned by the British Army. He was also held in great esteem by British meteorologists for whom he had built a kite in 1907 which could take a meteorograph to a great height. On one occasion the instrument, which registers wind speed and humidity levels, went up to 4275 metres, an achievement that earned Cody honorary membership of the Royal Meteorological Society.

Nevertheless, Cody was not really a high flyer. With his son, Leon, he always participated in kite competitions organized by various kite clubs throughout the country, but he never managed to win first prize. Usually this went to a certain Charles Brogden, the lucky owner of a mastodon with no fewer that six wings. All the same, Cody's kites always made the biggest impression, not only for their tremendous lift, but possibly even more because of their extraordinary construction. For Cody did not simply launch one kite at a time but would send up a whole fleet into the sky at once. First the so-called 'pilot kite', followed by the lifter kites, joined to the pilot kite by means of an ingenious sliding system on the towing strings, and finally the pièce de resistance, the carrier kite.
The carrier kite was joined to the lorry which was pulled along the cable of the pilot kite on wheels and in which the soldier Moreton went up 800 metres with no parachute or ejector seat. Quite a fellow.

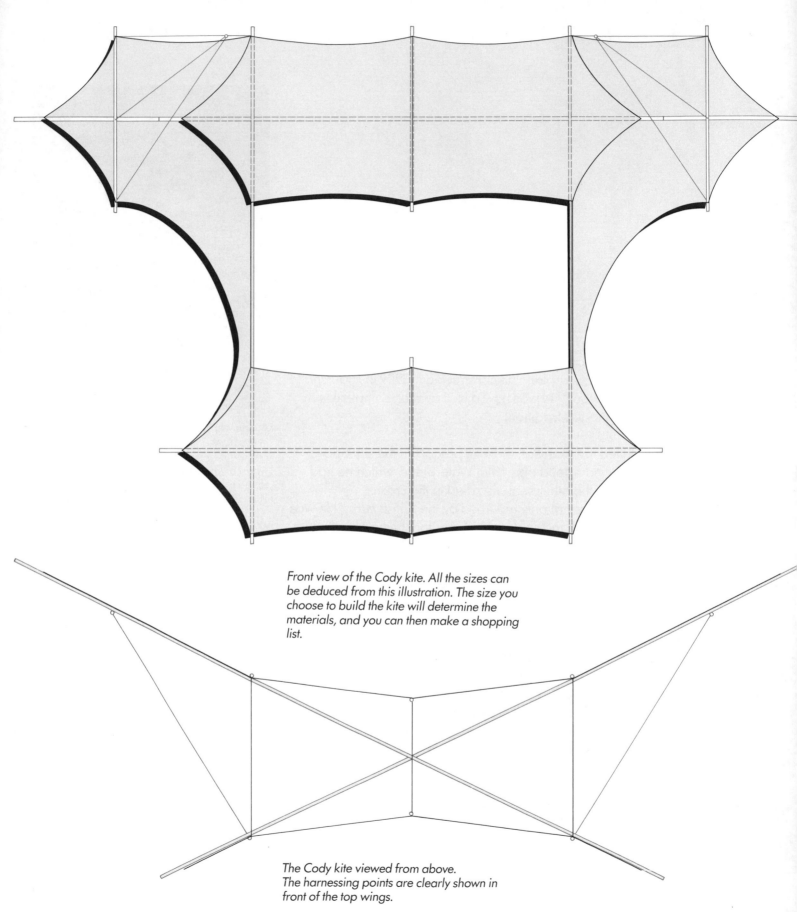

Front view of the Cody kite. All the sizes can be deduced from this illustration. The size you choose to build the kite will determine the materials, and you can then make a shopping list.

The Cody kite viewed from above. The harnessing points are clearly shown in front of the top wings.

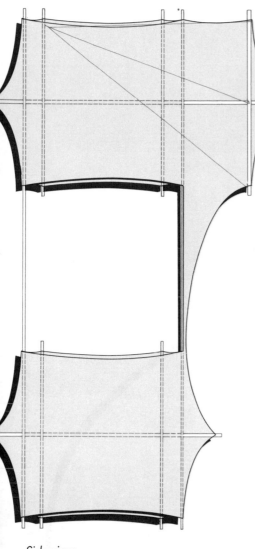

Side view.

Fixing the bridle

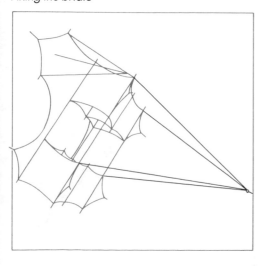

Construction.

The amount of material bought for this kite depends entirely on the size you wish to build it. We built a kite 7 ft tall with a span of 10 ft 20.

To build this kite you will need: over 30 square feet of spinnaker cloth and 21 yard of stick with a diameter of 0.4, 0.8 and 2 inch respectively. Before starting it's a good idea to make up a shopping list after studying the illustrations on these pages. If you decide to construct the cells 16 inch high, you can work out the other sizes in relation to the sizes given in the example. The cross-spars should be thicker than the vertical sticks.

Start by copying the patterns of the cells, wings, reinforcing struts and tunnels exactly onto paper, except for the curved parts of the wings, which should be copied onto thicker pieces of card. This can then be used for cutting the cloth when all the pattern pieces have been cut out. Then use a stapler to staple all the pieces together, checking that all the sizes are correct. Now you're ready to stitch the pieces together. Do double rows of stitching and use a tape of synthetic material to hem the cloth. This should be stitched on when the fabric is stretched over the frame, to prevent any folds or creases in the covering. The cells are attached to the covering by means of loops, and to the vertical sticks with cord. The lower wings have loops which fit into the groves notched into the ends of the sticks. The upper wings should also be fitted with cords through the same loops and grooves. Try to keep everything as symmetrical as possible. The sticks can be collapsible if aluminium tubes are used. The cylinders of the vertical spars should be as compact as possible, while the tunnels of the cross-spars can be rather larger.

The illustrations indicate how and where the reinforcements struts should be filled. The bridle on the upper wings is filled on the side. When the bridle is pulled tighter or relaxed, the kite will respond by moving smoothly or jerkily. Cody designed a number of different wings. The curved lines do not necessarily mean that there will be a better lift, but they do give this special, as well as historic kite, its own particular charm.

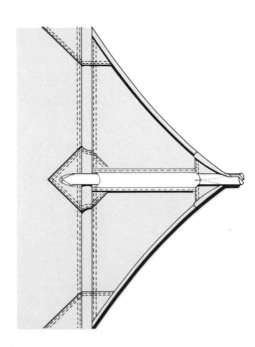

The position of the tunnels for the cross-spars.

The points of the wing in the bottom of the cross spar.

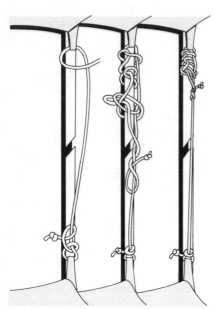

An example showing how the cells are fitted in relation to each other.

A clear pattern for the curve of the wing. This illustration also shows the places where reinforcing struts and tunnels can be fitted.

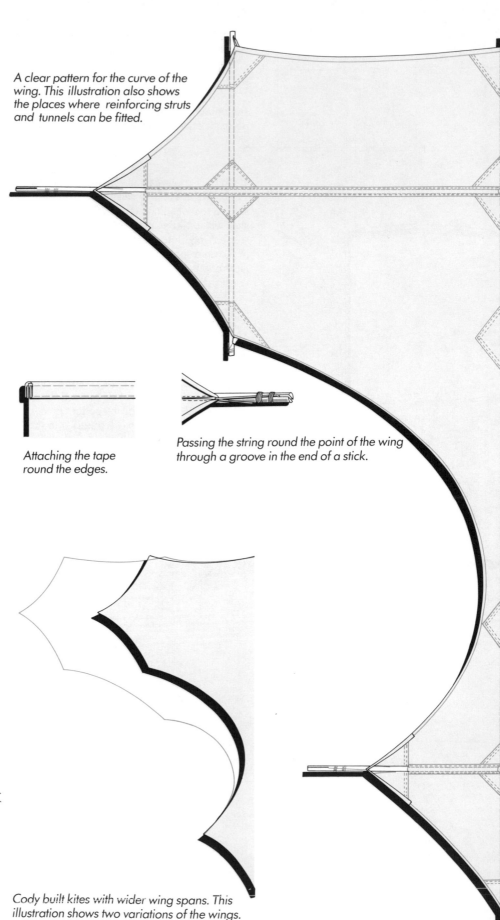

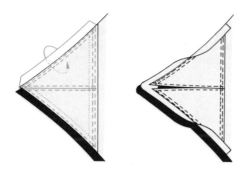

There is a lot of pressure on the tips of the wings and therefore they should be double stitched and finished off with tape.

Attaching the tape round the edges.

Passing the string round the point of the wing through a groove in the end of a stick.

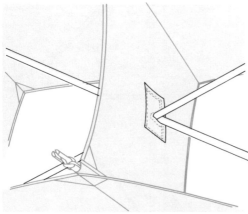

The cross-spars are passed through the central section of the cells. This therefore needs to be reinforced.

Cody built kites with wider wing spans. This illustration shows two variations of the wings.

One of the less well known, the Cody Compound, but by no means less interesting kites built by the grand master of kite building, Samuel Franklin Cody.

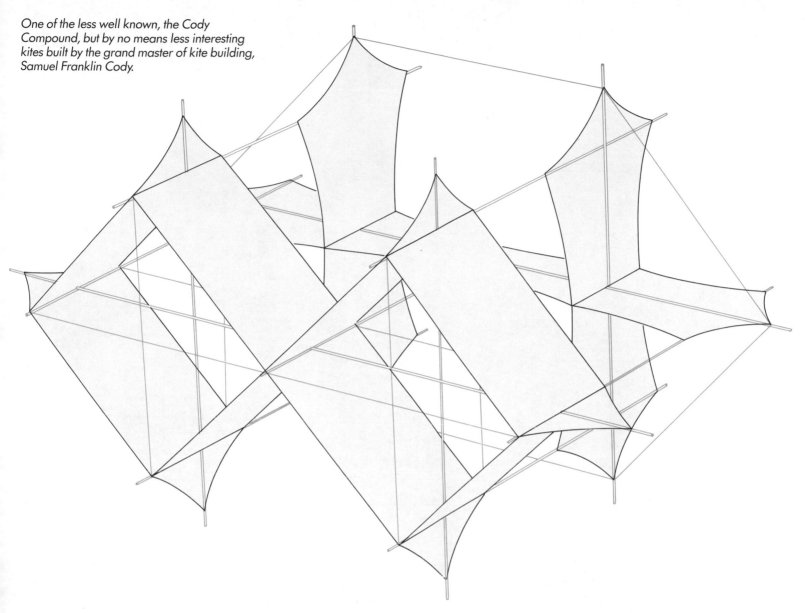

The cells are fixed to the vertical spars in a simple but efficient way, using loops made of spinnaker cloth.

The other side of the vertical spar is always held taut with string.

A string which goes round a stick halfway through the covering. At this point the fabric obviously needs some reinforcement.

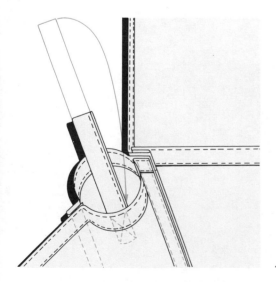

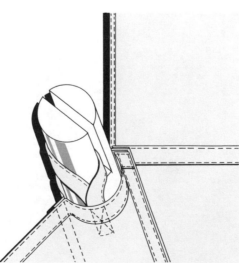

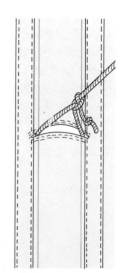

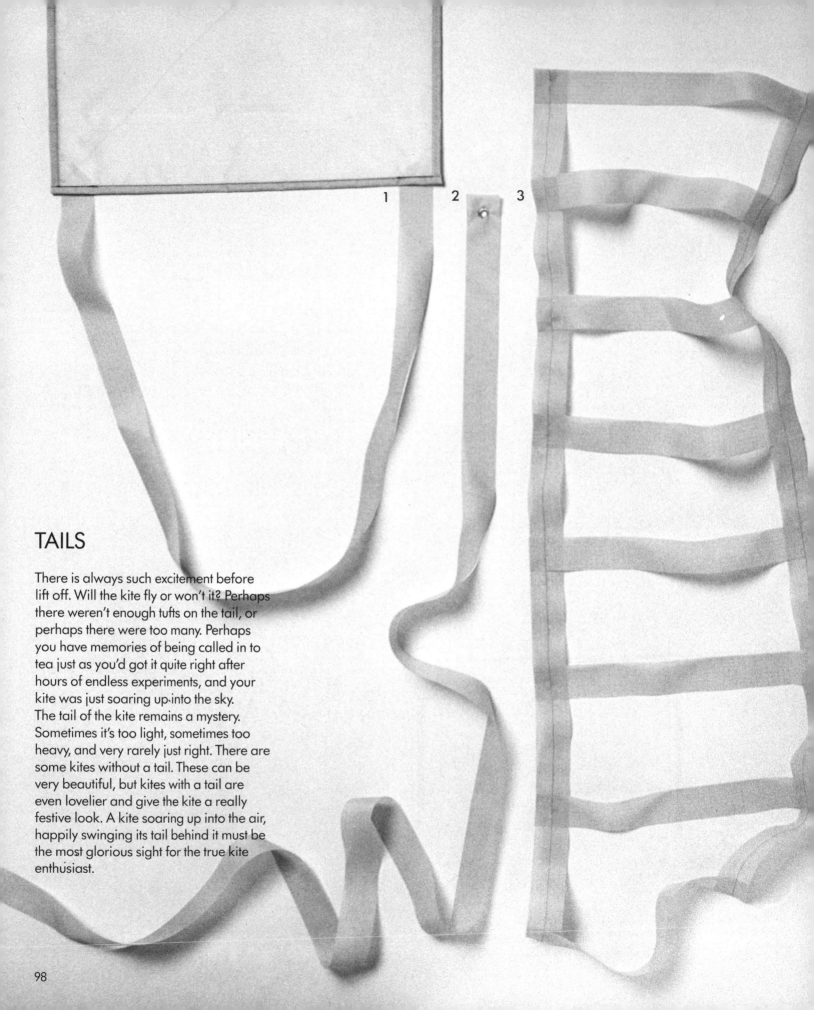

1   2   3

TAILS

There is always such excitement before
lift off. Will the kite fly or won't it? Perhaps
there weren't enough tufts on the tail, or
perhaps there were too many. Perhaps
you have memories of being called in to
tea just as you'd got it quite right after
hours of endless experiments, and your
kite was just soaring up into the sky.
The tail of the kite remains a mystery.
Sometimes it's too light, sometimes too
heavy, and very rarely just right. There are
some kites without a tail. These can be
very beautiful, but kites with a tail are
even lovelier and give the kite a really
festive look. A kite soaring up into the air,
happily swinging its tail behind it must be
the most glorious sight for the true kite
enthusiast.

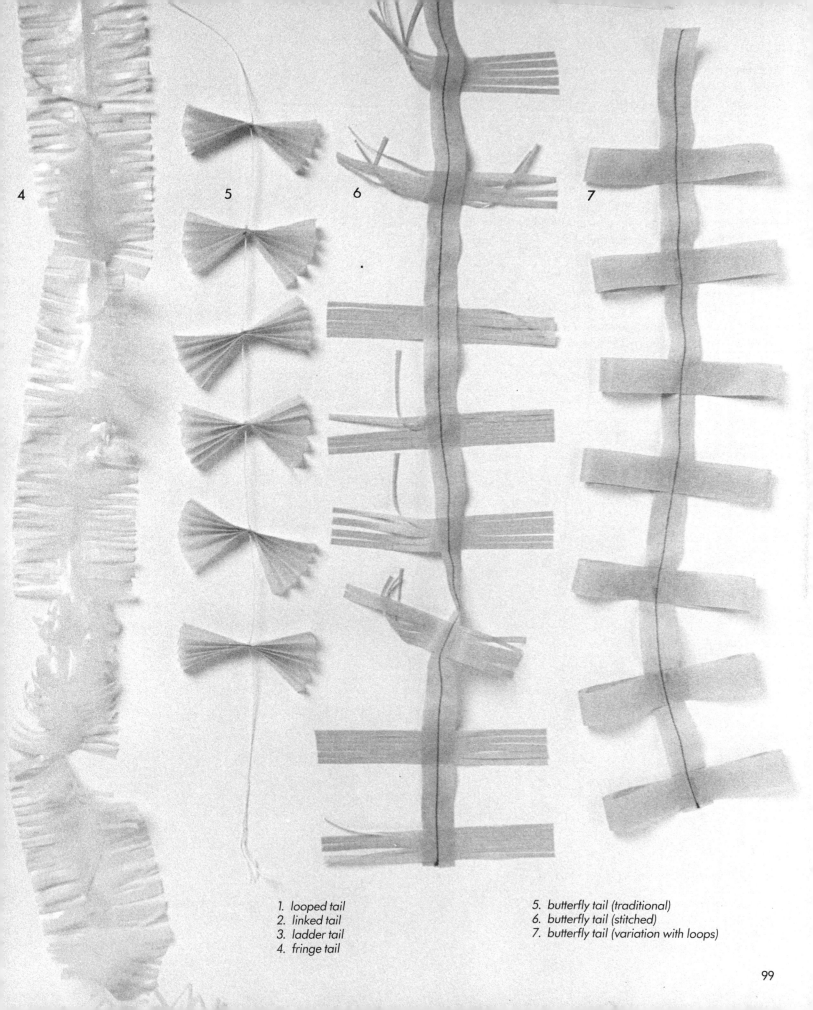

4

5

6

7

1. looped tail
2. linked tail
3. ladder tail
4. fringe tail

5. butterfly tail (traditional)
6. butterfly tail (stitched)
7. butterfly tail (variation with loops)

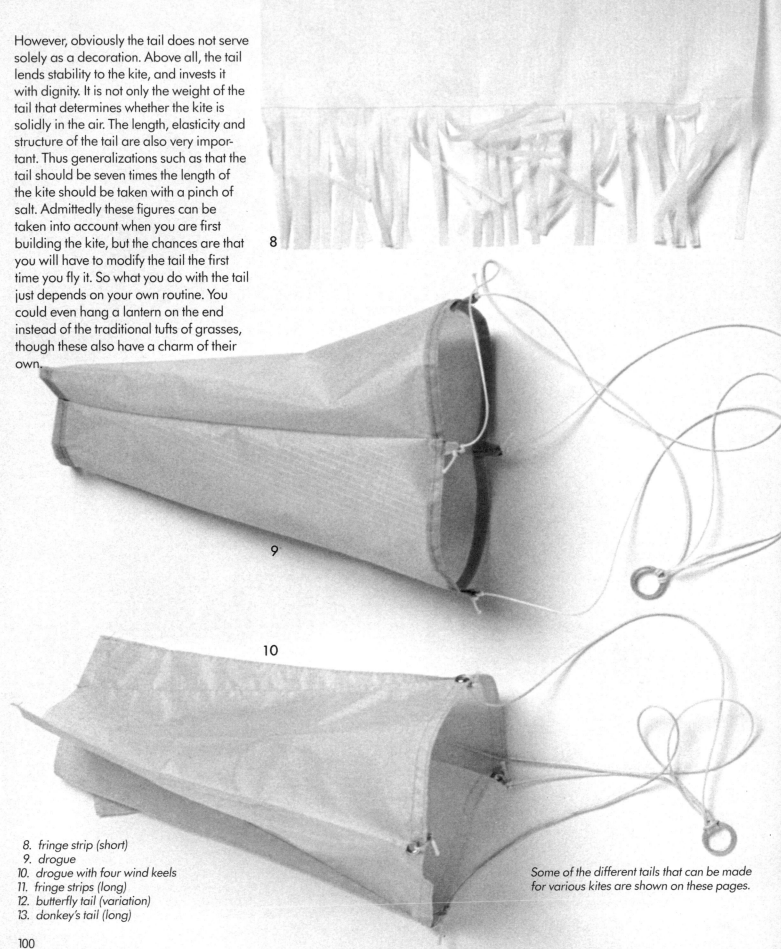

However, obviously the tail does not serve solely as a decoration. Above all, the tail lends stability to the kite, and invests it with dignity. It is not only the weight of the tail that determines whether the kite is solidly in the air. The length, elasticity and structure of the tail are also very important. Thus generalizations such as that the tail should be seven times the length of the kite should be taken with a pinch of salt. Admittedly these figures can be taken into account when you are first building the kite, but the chances are that you will have to modify the tail the first time you fly it. So what you do with the tail just depends on your own routine. You could even hang a lantern on the end instead of the traditional tufts of grasses, though these also have a charm of their own.

8

9

10

8. fringe strip (short)
9. drogue
10. drogue with four wind keels
11. fringe strips (long)
12. butterfly tail (variation)
13. donkey's tail (long)

Some of the different tails that can be made for various kites are shown on these pages.

11   12   13

REELS

What does the reel look like, and what should it look like? Reels come in all shapes and sizes and even the most comprehensive dictionary won't describe them all, though it cannot be denied that the entry under 'reel' gives an extremely detailed description of this essential piece of kite flying equipment.

The word 'reel' is defined in the Shorter Oxford English Dictionary as follows: '1. A rotary instrument on which thread is wound after it is spun, or silk as it is drawn from cocoons. 2. An apparatus by which a cord, line etc. may be wound up or unwound as required. 3. A small cylinder on which any flexible substance is wound.'

Whether or not this will help is anybody's guess. This stands to reason, because of all the bits and pieces you need to fly your kite, the reel must be the clumsiest, strangest and most difficult piece of equipment to use. Of course, it's always possible to resort to a stick, a tin can or a bottle, but a good reel will give you even more fun flying your kite. You feel more in tune with the soaring, wheeling object in the sky, and when you find you're in trouble, the reel is really useful. There's simply no easier way of taking in the kite quickly, for example, if it's suddenly attacked by gusts of wind, rain or other unforeseen weather conditions.
This actually means that the reel has to be sound and of good quality. Reels which

Left: a reel, as has been used since long times past. Right a more modern version with a progressive handle and — to make it even easier — supplied with a stick.
Bottom left: a special reel that can be attached to a belt.

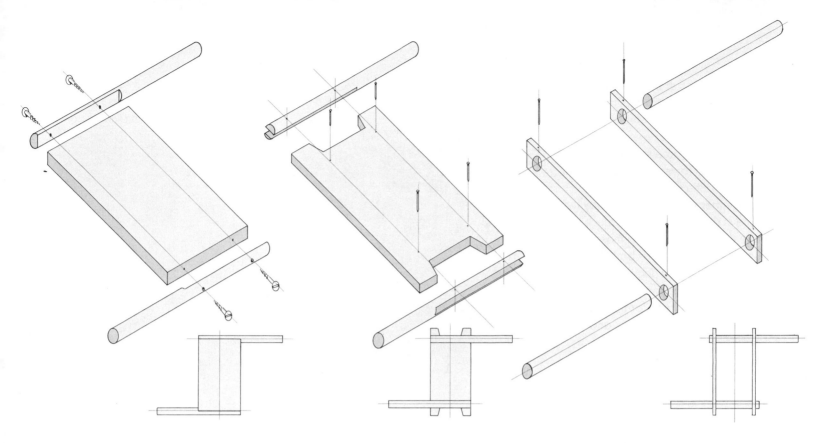

fall apart when you take in the kite don't do much for the kite flyer's enjoyment. What's worse, you may even lose the kite which you've worked so hard to make and which might be your pride and joy.

The diameter of a reel should not be too large.
Some real kite experts will immediately insist that the larger the reel, the fewer movements you will have to make to bring in the kite. A drum with a diameter of 10 inch makes it possible to bring in 30 inch of line with every turn. If the diameter is only 2 inch, it will take about five turns to bring in the same length of line.
However, this doesn't necessarily mean that you should choose a reel with a very large central piece. You'll find that the larger the reel, the more difficult it'll be to turn. In other words, the size of your reel will depend very largely on how high you want to fly your kite.

More or less the same thing applies with regard to the solidity of the reel. But there is another consideration regarding this aspect of the reel, and that is windspeed.

Above: three standard types of conventional reels. Below: a reel, of which the spool runs on ball bearings.

Certainly when a stiff breeze is blowing, in particular when you're reeling in the kite, it's quite possible for the reel to fall apart like a house of cards.

What's the lesson to be learned from this? Perhaps it's best to use an electric motor as a reel, for little can go wrong with these. Whether you would still enjoy flying your kite is another matter. It's much better to make the reel but to keep it as simple as possible. This brings us back to square one, the stick, a bottle and a tin can. However, it just goes to show how difficult it is to find the right reel, for this simple model is rather difficult to use, and a pair of handles always comes in useful.

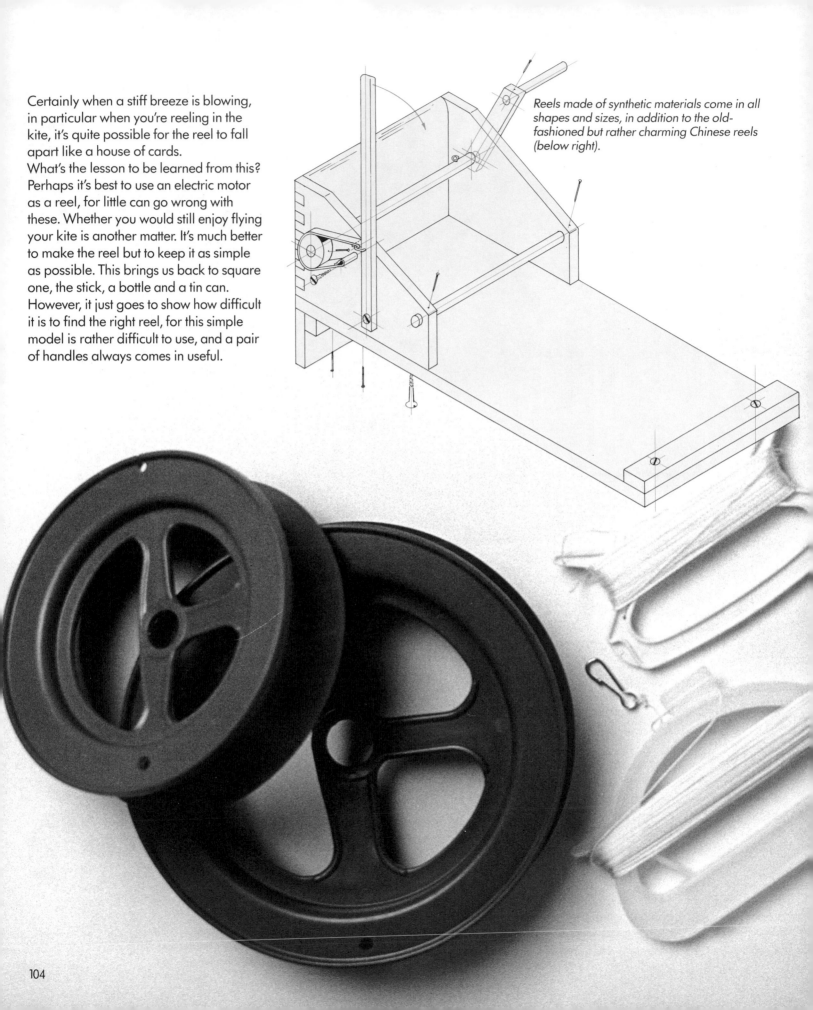

Reels made of synthetic materials come in all shapes and sizes, in addition to the old-fashioned but rather charming Chinese reels (below right).

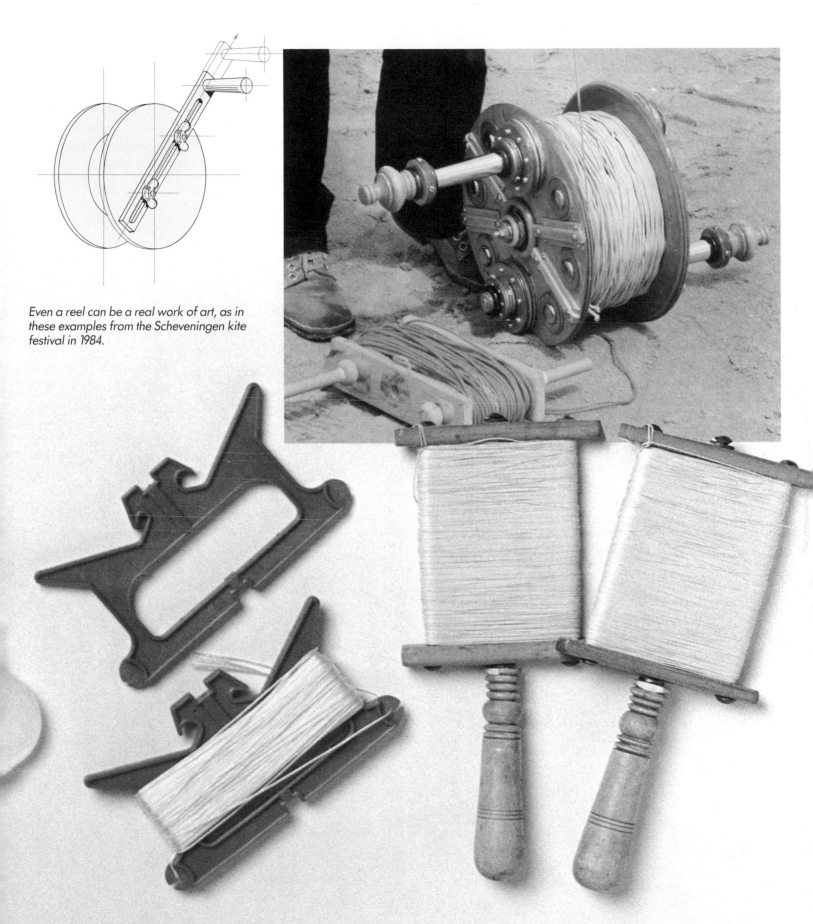

Even a reel can be a real work of art, as in these examples from the Scheveningen kite festival in 1984.

105

Thus reels come in just as many different shapes and sizes as the kites themselves. They are also just as easy or as difficult to make as you want them to be. However, you must remember that it is an important matter – don't be in a hurry simply because you can't wait to fly your kite. You could even ask for expert advice, although you might find that an expert would go on and on about reels and connections, cogs and all the other paraphernalia which have been dreamed up through the ages. In the United States they have even used the mechanism of fishing reels, and the lines which were once used to catch tuna fish are now used to fly kites.

There are literally hundreds of reels.

106

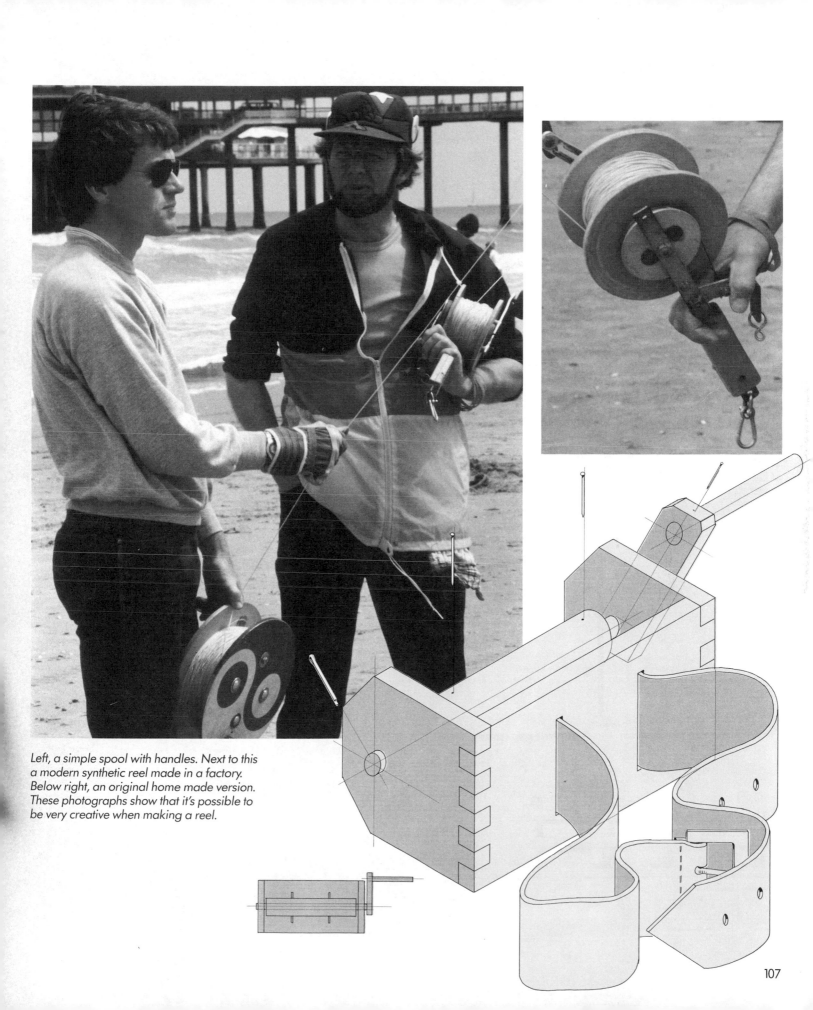

Left, a simple spool with handles. Next to this
a modern synthetic reel made in a factory.
Below right, an original home made version.
These photographs show that it's possible to
be very creative when making a reel.

MESSENGER KITES

Finally your work of art is complete and with a slight tug to the right or an occasional pull to the left you are ready to fly your kite, and see it as a statue against the blue firmament. The kite of your dreams, steady as a rock, a haven of peace in the chaos of life – a monument.

But thought it may be beautiful, it's easy to become bored. After watching the thing proudly with tears in your eyes, the boredom sets in. If kite flying is to continue being fun, the sport must have its spectacular aspects, and this really isn't too difficult to achieve. For example, try sending a message by kite, make it snow or try sending up a light.

It's quite possible to try these tricks with a plain and straightforward kite. If you're feeling really ambitious, have a go at aerial photography, although it's not advisable to start with this straightaway.

Begin by sending simple telegrams, sheets of paper with a hole in the middle, which are attached to the flying line in such a way that they are taken up into the air, chased by the wind.

Once you have mastered this technique, send up bags of confetti. A simple technical trick makes it possible to open the bags just at the point they are near the kite, and you'll see it start to snow. There are also endless possibilities with paper aeroplanes and parachutes.
From this you can progress to cameras or even cine cameras. This will almost inevitably cost you a few films, but once you succeed, you'll find that some of the results will be well worthwhile. An aerial photograph – or even better, an aerial film of you flying your kite – it's certainly different.

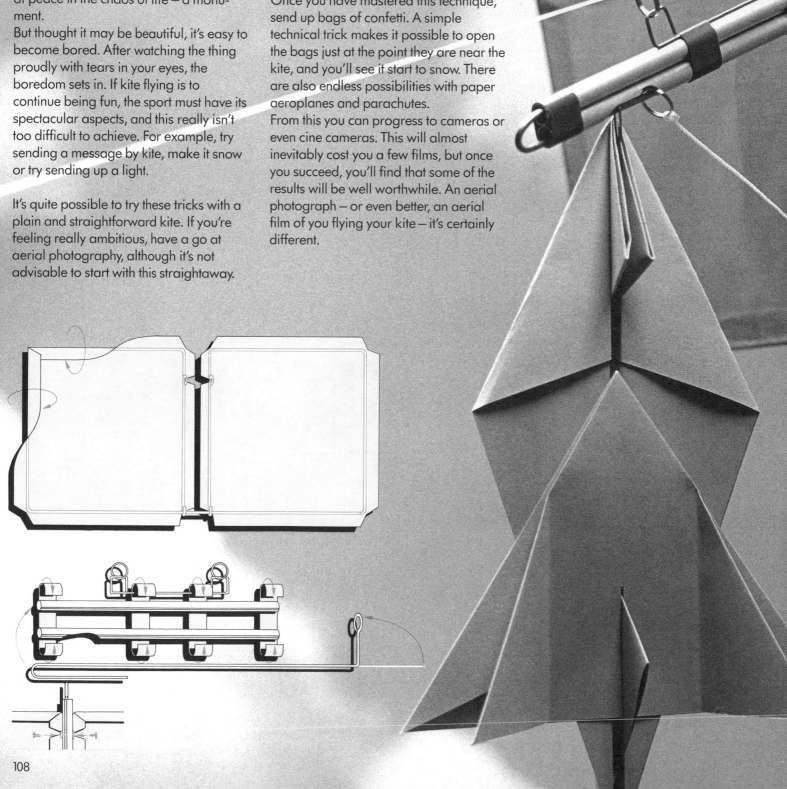

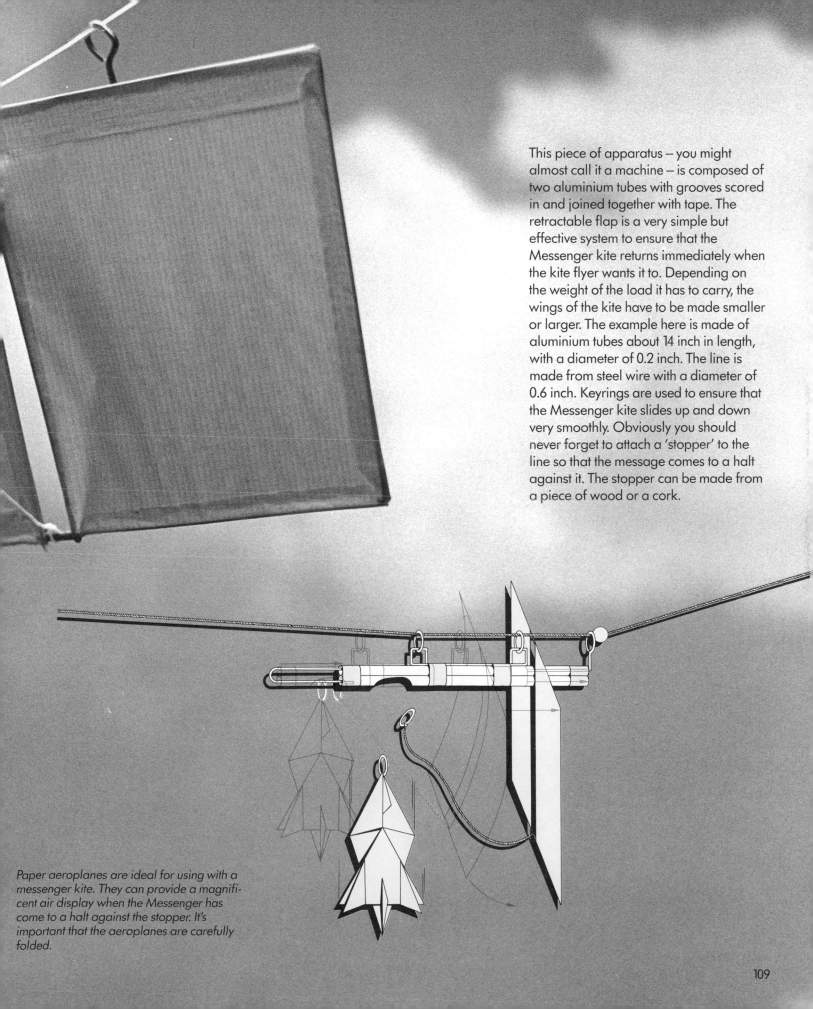

This piece of apparatus — you might almost call it a machine — is composed of two aluminium tubes with grooves scored in and joined together with tape. The retractable flap is a very simple but effective system to ensure that the Messenger kite returns immediately when the kite flyer wants it to. Depending on the weight of the load it has to carry, the wings of the kite have to be made smaller or larger. The example here is made of aluminium tubes about 14 inch in length, with a diameter of 0.2 inch. The line is made from steel wire with a diameter of 0.6 inch. Keyrings are used to ensure that the Messenger kite slides up and down very smoothly. Obviously you should never forget to attach a 'stopper' to the line so that the message comes to a halt against it. The stopper can be made from a piece of wood or a cork.

Paper aeroplanes are ideal for using with a messenger kite. They can provide a magnificent air display when the Messenger has come to a halt against the stopper. It's important that the aeroplanes are carefully folded.

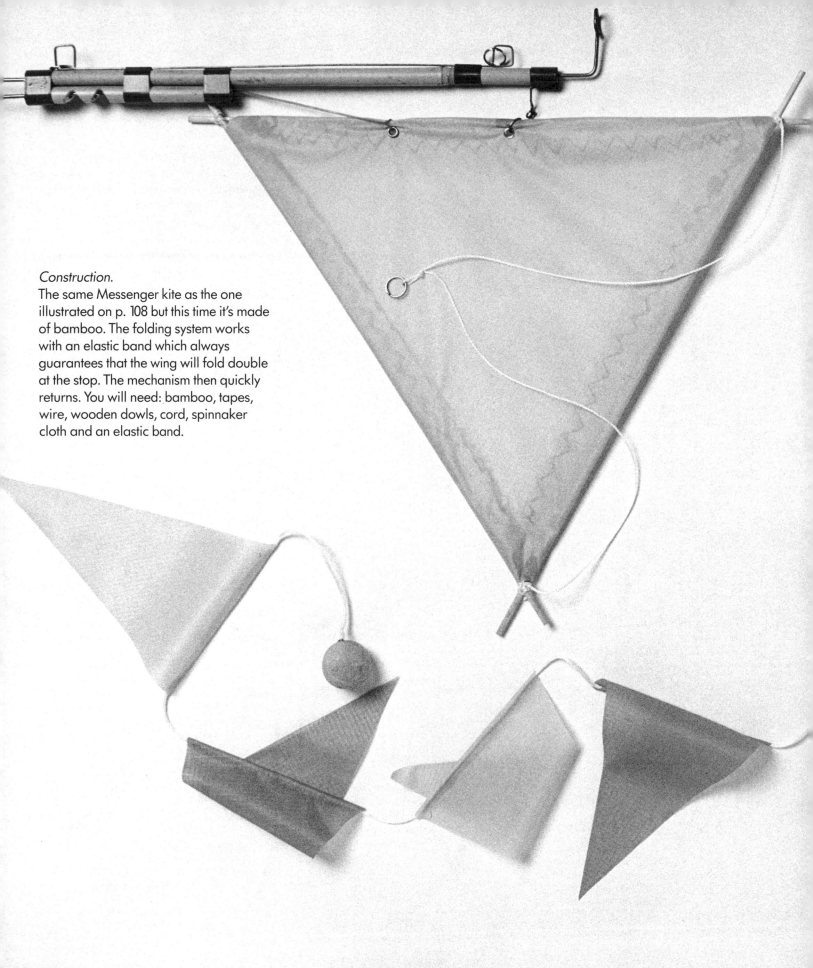

Construction.
The same Messenger kite as the one illustrated on p. 108 but this time it's made of bamboo. The folding system works with an elastic band which always guarantees that the wing will fold double at the stop. The mechanism then quickly returns. You will need: bamboo, tapes, wire, wooden dowls, cord, spinnaker cloth and an elastic band.

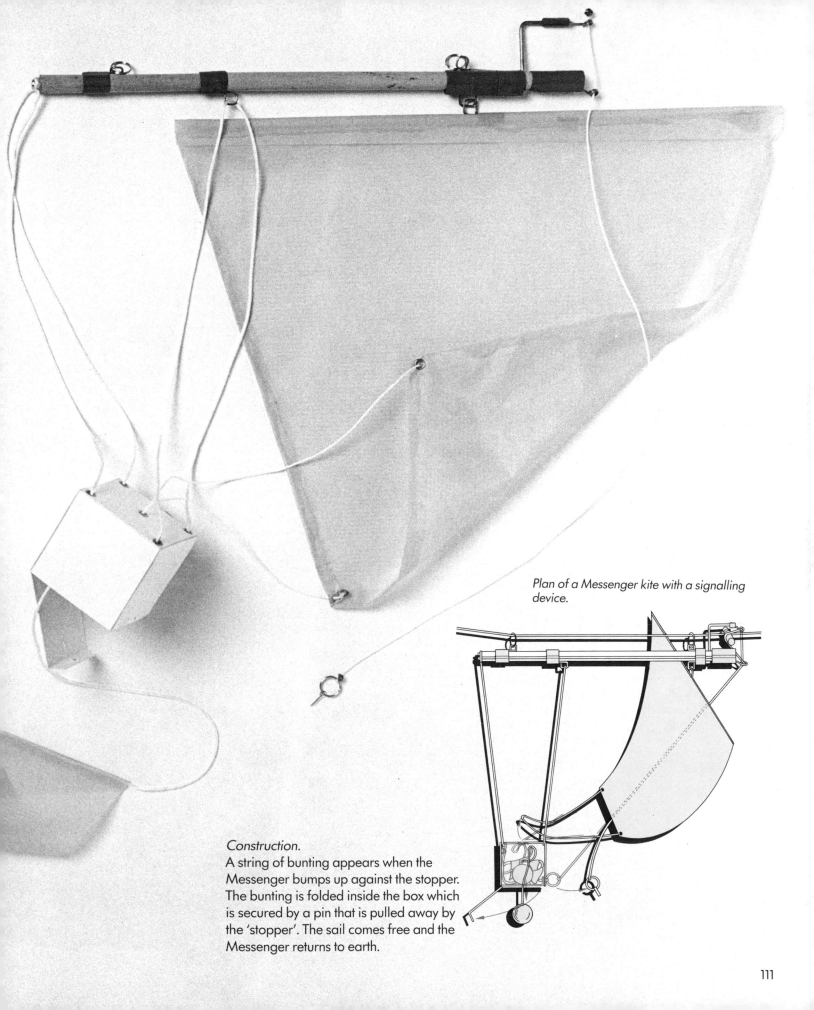

Plan of a Messenger kite with a signalling device.

Construction.
A string of bunting appears when the Messenger bumps up against the stopper. The bunting is folded inside the box which is secured by a pin that is pulled away by the 'stopper'. The sail comes free and the Messenger returns to earth.

An ingenious device consisting of a mousetrap as the basis of this very special messenger. You can actually use it to send a camera up into the air to take photographs of yourself. It's fairly obvious that it's best to send up a cheap and, above all, quite light camera because you can never be sure about what might happen. The camera and mousetrap are activated by the stopper. The sail shuts and then the mechanism slides back down. If you wish, you can wind on the film and make another attempt at taking a picture. It's a good idea to make another 'stopper' just in front of the reel. The camera could otherwise return so quickly that you could end up with a bruised thumb. Use a cork which you can slide up and down the line.

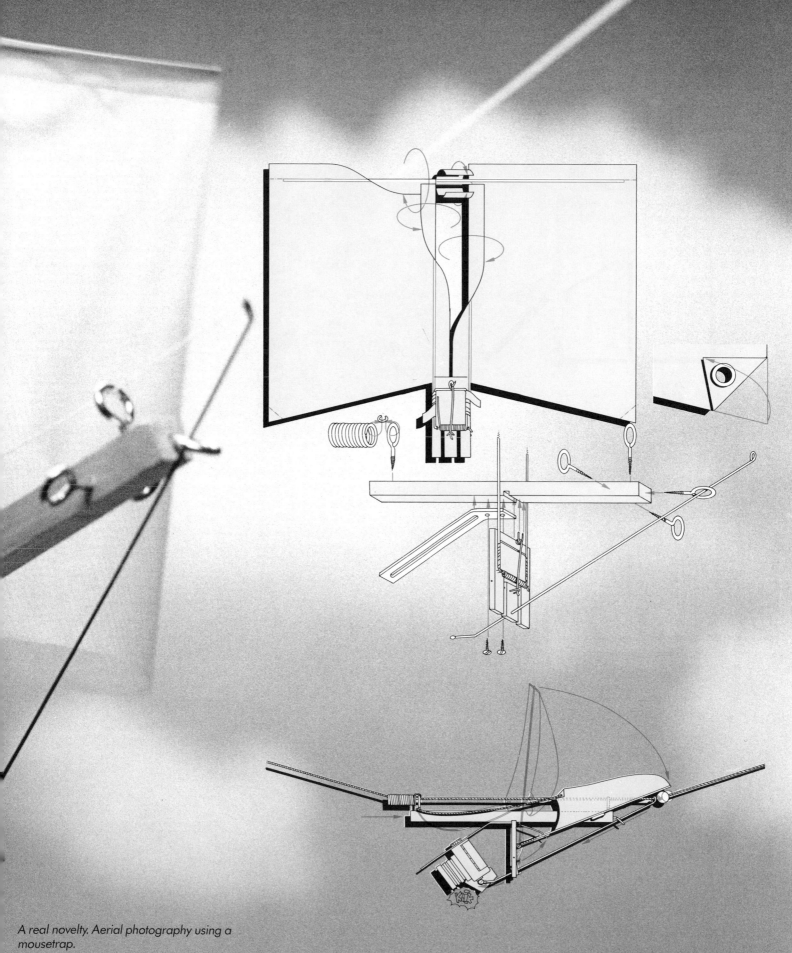

A real novelty. Aerial photography using a mousetrap.

FOLDED KITES

Simple and effective. Fold a sheet of
construction paper in two, cut off the
edges, attach a small bridle and you
have the simplest kite that was ever made.

A sled. All you need is a sheet of paper
folded into a harmonica shape, and a
small bridle.

Parasled. Another sheet of construction
paper folded double and stapled
together on the bottom.

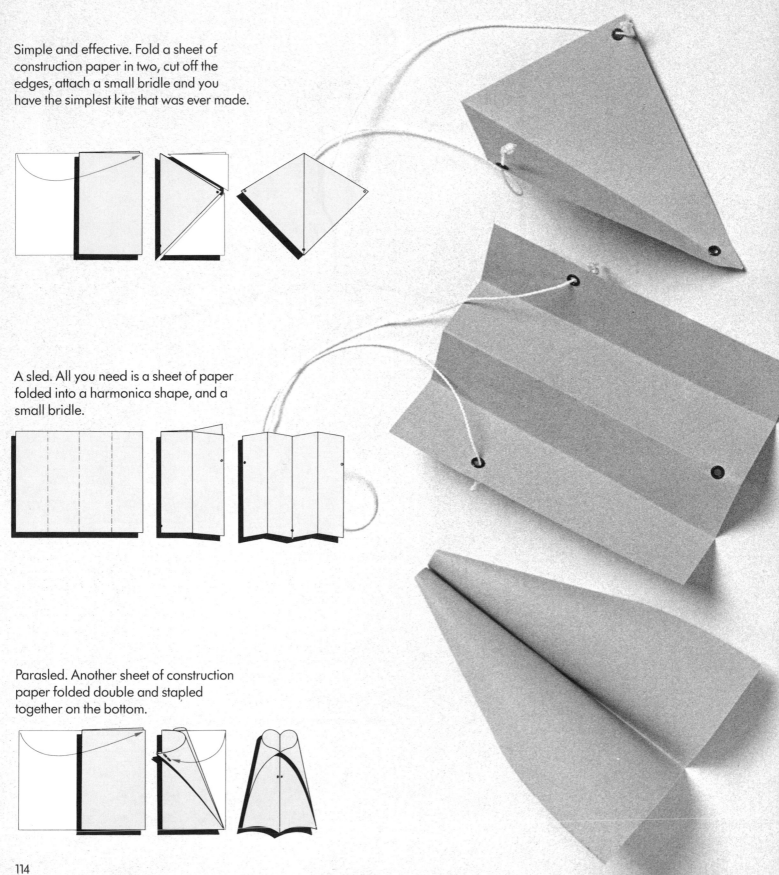

You can make a kite with a keel bridle by cutting out two pieces of paper according to the pattern and sticking them together.

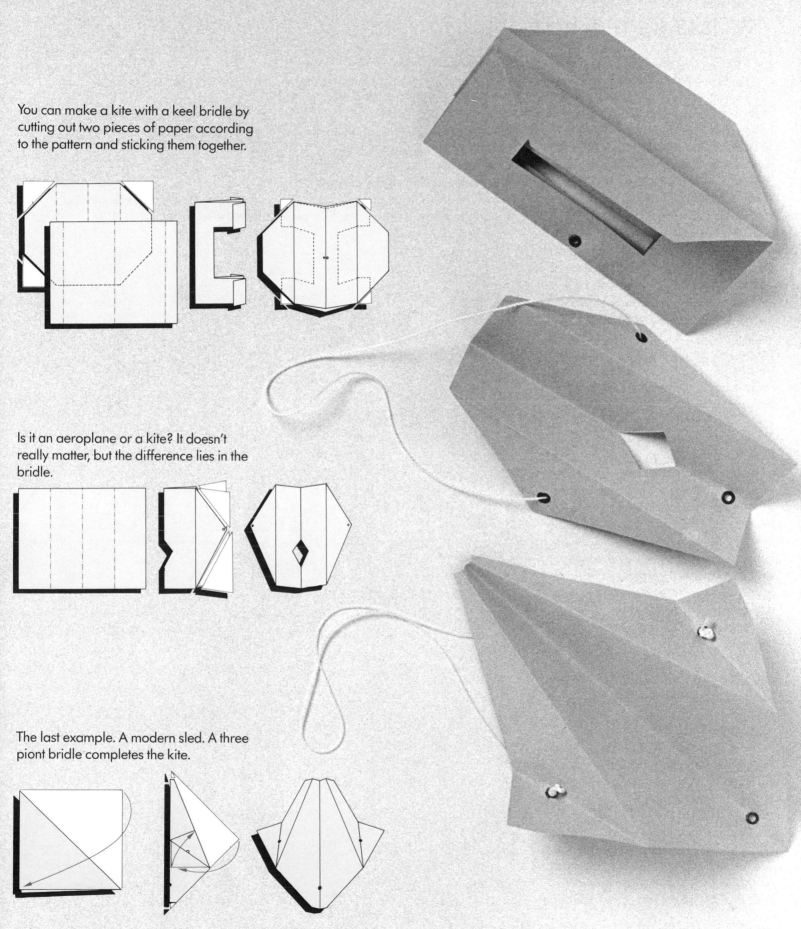

Is it an aeroplane or a kite? It doesn't really matter, but the difference lies in the bridle.

The last example. A modern sled. A three piont bridle completes the kite.

TRIMMING THE KITE

Just like a sailing boat, your kite should in theory skim like a seagull over the waves. However, in practice it may not always be quite like this. The boat still needs to be trimmed, or adjusted to size. The mast may have to be moved a fraction backwards or forewards, the main sail may have to balloon out slightly more. These subtle modifications can turn the ship into a real winner.

Kites are just the same. They should also be adjusted, first at home, and later on, outside as well.
'Trimming' the kite at home will not be an exceptionally precise affair, but it'll certainly help a bit. It'll no longer be necessary to make so many modifications to your kite, which may well be rather difficult to handle when there is a stiff breeze.

Starting at home, first lie your kite on the floor with the bridle facing upwards, and pull it up with the index finger under the bridle line. If the kite is properly balanced it won't tip over. If it does tip, balance the left and right halves by shaving a splinter off the cross-spar on the side which is too heavy. Don't start shaving splinters off straightaway because before you know it, you'll find you've shaved off too much and you'll have to start shaving on the other side. It's quite possible to end up without a kite at all.

Once you've got the balance right let the kite dangle from the same finger in such a way that the bottom is slightly lower than the top. The angle of the kite in relation to the floor is about 25 degrees. If the kite is hanging still, as it should be, the finger is pointing at the spot where the ring should be attached.

You're ready to take the kite out for the 'finishing touches'. Send the kite up but don't let the line out more than about 20 inch. If the kite goes up immediately and stays just above your head, the bridle

ring should be slid up a little. Once the ring is right the kite will pull up the line at an angle, properly balanced.

If the kite is still wavering, make a note of which way it tends to go. It is then necessary to correct the balance. If the kite wobbles to the left and the right, try to make it more stable by giving it a tail, or by making the tail longer.

Angle of bridle lines for different wind conditions.

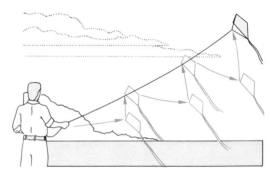

Method of letting out and pulling back the line when there's little wind.

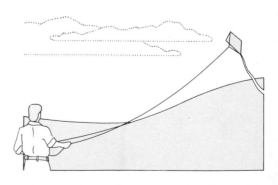

A better place to fly your kite when there's little wind – in the lee of a hill.

FLYING A KITE

When you're building your kite as well as when you're actually flying it, you should always remember the rather tedious fact that a kite is heavier than air. The kite will only rise up into the air due to a clever combination of dastardly tricks. If you forget about any of the tricks, things inevitably go wrong, with the unhappy result that in most cases the kite will plummet down to the ground and crash. In fact, it might even be worse than that. So this chapter of kite flying technique is by no means an unimportant section of the book.

The technique starts with building the kite, and the first thing to look at is the bridle. The bridle ensures that the kite flies at a particular angle in relation to the wind. If this is the right angle, the upward pressure means that the kite will stay up in the air – if it's the wrong angle, even a small child can guess what the outcome will be.
However, it is not the case that the angle has to be precisely 12°, for example, which is just as well.
You would virtually have to be an engineer specialising in aerodynamics to build a bridle complying with all the requirements if this were actually the case. Still, it is obvious that you cannot simply build or repair a bridle based on pure guesswork. You must keep to the fundamental rules and adapt the bridle to the wind conditions.

Obviously there are other factors influencing the kite's flight, if it has been constructed correctly. The resistance of the flying line is one aspect; the extent to which the kite is bowed (which will also provide some lift at the back of the kite) is another factor. However if all these considerations were to be discussed the book would turn into a list of complicated instructions, and that is certainly not our intention.

The next thing to deal with is the stability of the kite. For most basic kites you won't encounter any problems. You must remember that if the width is too great in proportion to the length, the kite will be very difficult to stabilise, even for an expert kite flyer. Of course, you can experiment endlessly with the tail. Do you remember the old fashioned way with a tuft of grass added to the tail, and then another taken away? However, as kite flying professors learned many years ago, the weight of the tail has nothing to do with the stability of the kite. Only the length affects this.

What do you do when the kite has no tail at all? There are other methods which can be used, and there are all sorts of possibilities. A hole in the right place can work wonders, but the beginner should not pay too much attention to this unless he has an extremely precise plan of his kite.

The same applies more or less to attaching small rudders, keels, fins or whatever else you choose to call these minor attachments. However, it's quite possible to affix these in all sorts of places on the front, the back, or anywhere else on the body of the kite. It's not very easy, and really it's best to try a small drogue or – the most usual method of all – by bowing the cross-spar.

The drogue or windbag is a small pointed bottomless bag made of fabric (see p. 100). This drogue makes a perfect tail, but there are plenty of kite flyers who don't like it because they think it makes the kite look ugly. This is a point of contention, but it is unquestionably true that the best way of stabilising a kite is to alter the curve of the cross-spar by bending it to a greater or lesser extent. The extent to which the cross-spar is bent actually determines the stability of the kite, and the best way to find out is to fly your kite a few times.

So after a lot of blood, sweat and tears, you'll finally be ready to fly your kite for the first time. Where's the best place to take it? Obviously you'll choose a place where the chance of crashing your kite is minimal. A flat expanse of land is quite ideal. Any playing field, meadow or beach is a perfect terrain for the kite flyers.

However, it's not always possible to find a meadow or a beach just round the corner. If this is the case, choose the spot to fly your kite very carefully. For example, never go anywhere near electricity lines or pylons. It shouldn't really be necessary to mention this, but there are always people who throw caution to the wind when flying their kites. Even nylon line can give a kite flyer a very nasty shock – especially if it's wet – if the kite flies into an overhead power line.

Nor is it advisable to fly your kite over a freeway or any other busy road; even the most stable kite can sometimes take an unexpected nose dive, and this could have very unfortunate consequences for an unsuspecting motorist, motorcyclist, or anyone else on the road.

Few people know that it is forbidden to fly a kite within 3 miles of an airfield. You may also not fly a kite heavier than 4.25 lb or at a height of more than 24 inch.

So you must keep away from electricity pylons and overhead lines, motorways, airports, as well as railways and blocks of houses, because of the strange gusts of wind. What's left? It's always possible to find somewhere, even if the land isn't absolutely flat. A low hill can sometimes be extremely suitable. In this case you shouldn't go right to the top of the hill, although you often see people trying this. On the other hand, don't go too far from the top, so that the kite can take advantage of the rising air as long as you remain on the windy side.

You now have a good kite, you've found the right place, and it really is time to fly the kite. You take the line in your hands your assistant is standing a little way off, holding the kite. You shout, 'Ready!' and start running as fast as you can, holding the line in your hand in the traditional manner.

However, this is all wrong. Apart from the fact that you might well trip up while you're running backwards, and could hit your head on something, it's also possible that you'll pull the kite right into the ground with all this uncontrolled activity. You'll end up with a hole in the head and a kite consisting of kindling and tattered paper, and possibly even a length of line embedded in the skin of the palm of your hand.

Obviously there is a better way. Hold the kite at the point where the line is attached to the bridle, let the wind play with the kite and feel it pull. At the moment that it really tugs hard, let out the line slightly. If it doesn't tug so hard, hold the line very tight and firm; in this way the kite will gradually go up very high. It's a matter of give and take. Do make sure that the line is attached to a reel or at least to a stick as it is quite possible to get a very unpleasant shock if you try to let out a line which is not attached to anything at the end. Before you know where you are, you'll find yourself with two empty hands.

Another way to fly your kite is to find a helper to assist you. It's his job to get the kite up, draping the tail in such a way over the ground that it cannot become tangled when it goes up into the air, while you stand forty or fifty yards further on with the wind behind you. Give a sign that he can let go of the kite, and at the same time pull strongly and evenly on the line. If you get it right, the kite will go flying up into the air like a rocket, and moreover, it will stay in a particular place. Once the kite is up, you can then start letting out

line if there is enough of a pull on the kite. When it starts to lose heights, pull in the line a bit.

Be a neat kite flyer, i.e., make sure that you always have control over the line. Don't let the kite go off course too much when you pull it in. Wind it around the reel or even around your elbow straight-away. There's no job more tedious than untangling a kite line while the kite is still up in the air. An unexpected movement – like bending over – could even result in your kite returning to earth.

PHOTOCREDITS

Botermans, Jack: pages 1, 2, 3, 9, 14 below, 63, 68, 82, 83.
Delft, Pieter van: page 14 below.
Dijk, David van: all other photo's.
Early Aviation at Farnborough, Percy B. Walker: page 12, 86, 87, 88, 89, 91.
Hoogerdijk, Jaap: page 93.
Lartique, Jacques Henri: page 6.
Pronk, Pete: pages 90, 91.

BIBLIOGRAPHY

Kite and Kite Flying Hamlyn Publishing Group

Kites David Pelham

Vliegers zelf maken Harm van Veen

Cerfs-volants Didier Carpentier / Joël Bachelet

Vliegers maken André Thiebault

Early Aviation at Farnborough Percy B. Walker

The complete Book of Kites and Kiteflying Will Yolen

The Art of the Japanese Kite Tal Streeter

Drachen bauen Werner Backes

Vlieger Stichting Nederlandse vliegerpromotie, The Hague, Holland

Nederlands vliegergezelschap, Maastricht, Holland